The Tween Scene

A Year of Programs for 10- to 14-Year-Olds

Tiffany Balducci and
Brianne Wilkins-Bester

VOYA Press

an imprint of E L Kurdyla Publishing, LLC

Bowie, Maryland

ISBN 978-1-61751-029-8

Copyright © 2014

Published by VOYA Press, an imprint of E L Kurdyla Publishing LLC

LCCN: 2014948979

The paper used in this publication meets the minimum requirements of the American National Standard for Information Sciences-Permanence of Paper for Printed Materials, ANSI Z39.48-1992.

Printed in the United States of America

Table of Contents

Acknowledgements

We would like to thank Dinah Gough and Oshawa Public Libraries for giving two young librarians the opportunity to create and implement groundbreaking tween programs and for encouraging us to extend the boundaries of traditional library services.

The Tween Scene: A Year of Programs for 10- to 14-Year-Olds is a compilation of many tried and true programs that would not be possible without the help and advice of our co-workers, the support of library management and the library board, and sustained funding from the City of Oshawa. We would especially like to thank Kim Powell for her innovative ideas and amazing enthusiasm for tween programming; Val Day for her calm, steadfast support and creativity; Jennifer Clark for her vision and dedication which made the 5th Grader and 8th Grade Grad programs a success; Gail Canonaco for her impressive inception and organization of the Mother-Daughter Bookclub; Candice Fischer and the graphics department for creating such eye-popping posters; and Spencer Haze for taking our ideas and brilliantly transforming them into the reproducibles found in this book.

We would also like to express gratitude and appreciation to RoseMary Honnold for her support and guidance as editor and for giving us a chance to write our first book.

Tiffany would like to thank her family for always supporting her love of reading and writing, especially her late grandfather, Richard Crane. She thanks her sisters, Chelsea and Bianca, who spent hours listening to made-up stories and were forced to act in the plays that she wrote. Tiffany would also like to acknowledge the support of her mentor, Ellen Stroud, for being "Far More Than You Expect!" And finally, she would like to acknowledge her friends and co-workers for their support and being a surrogate family.

Brianne would like to thank her elementary school librarian, Mary Wolff, for inspiring her to pursue a career in librarianship; her family, Brian, Margarethe, and Lindsay, for encouraging her lifelong dream; and her husband, Chris, for lovingly supporting her career decisions. She would also like to thank her colleagues for their friendship and for motivating her to step outside of her comfort zone. Finally, Brianne would like to express gratitude to Susan Downs, Marilyn Pillar, and the staff at Innisfil Public Library for giving the girl in blue suit a chance and for teaching her the ABCs of library programming.

Introduction:
Welcome to the Tween Scene

"Pre-pubescent," "Pre-adolescent," "Youth," "Pre-teen." These are a few of the terms used to describe individuals that are no longer children, but not yet teenagers. More recently, marketing gurus and librarians are using the word "tween." Much like its predecessors, the word "tween" also holds a rather ambiguous definition. There is no doubt that it defines the period between childhood and the teenage years, yet the question lies in the exact ages. Some suggest that the tween years begin at age eight and end at age fourteen, while others argue every age in between. For the purposes of this book, the term "tween" will refer to individuals aged ten to fourteen. It is important to note, though, that when planning your own tween programs, it makes sense to choose an age range that is appropriate to your local demographics, library mandate, and staff comfort level.

Tweens in Today's World

The newer term of "tween" has been popping up so much over the past few years due to the fact that this demographic has evolved and has quickly become a sophisticated group that impacts everything, from social media to consumerism to marketing campaigns. When consulting the vast array of articles and books, such as *Chasing Youth Culture and Getting It Right* (Wiley, 2007) and *Gen BuY* (Jossey-Bass, 2007), that focus on marketing to tweens, it is obvious that this is a hot topic and that the tween segment of the population is indeed powerful.

Not only are today's tweens and their parents spending a significant amount of money, some suggest up to $260 billion annually in the United States alone (Ginsburg), but they are also becoming more engaged citizens than Generation X (those born in the 60s and 70s). Perhaps it is a stronger sense of pressure and responsibility, as the tweens of today exhibit more concern about and must face many social issues including cyber bullying, terrorism, substance abuse, and self-image (Wells, p. 61). With the rise of social media, tweens are no longer protected from these weighty topics as they may have once been. Perhaps due to this fact, tweens are adopting a greater sense of identity, as is reflected in their almost teen- or adult-like sense of persona and style (Moore). In effect, they are sounding less like children and more like teens and adults (Wells, p.61).

Intellectual and Emotional Characteristics

When it comes to the human brain, researchers are now realizing that complete development does not occur until age twenty five, and that the part of the brain responsible for abstract thinking, impulse control, and understanding consequences (pre-frontal cortex) does not even start developing until age twelve (Holmes). As a result, tweens may require adult guidance in the areas of decision making and proper social behaviors, even if they are starting to question authority at the same time. To help tweens gain the confidence needed to make decisions and to conduct themselves properly, emphasize progress made from previous performance, refrain from comparing them to other tweens, and help them to identify their own strengths (Texas 4-H).

Another unique element in the tween brain is the amygdala, or emotional center, which is hyperactive in the adolescent years. This means that every thought, action, and statement gets an "extra helping of emotion" (Holmes), causing mood swings and the inability to express and interpret mental states. If tweens are getting overly emotional (angry, excited, sad, happy, etc.) at library programs and it is starting to affect others, encourage the emotional tween to take a moment, to breathe, and to collect their emotions before the situation escalates.

Finally, tween's brains are undergoing changes that will make it faster and more efficient. As a result, old and useless information is being discarded to make way for new growth and skills that will help tweens to succeed as adults. By repeatedly viewing and hearing appropriately modeled behavior from adults, tweens will acquire these skills more quickly.

Tweens need to be given the opportunity to participate in situations where they can develop and practice using these important emotional, reasoning, and decision making skills. They also need experiences to fulfill their need for excitement, thrills, and risks. And what better place than in the safety of a structured library program?

Physical Characteristics

As tweens begin to enter puberty, their bodies are undergoing a variety of changes, many of which result in anxiety, embarrassment, self-consciousness, and awkwardness. While some tweens are getting taller, others remain short; while some remain slight, others are filling out. Boys voices begin to change and crack. Body odor, oily skin, and acne become more obvious. Consequently, some tweens become more timid, comparing themselves to others and having a difficult time in group settings. In the library, it is important to be aware of these concerns and realize that some tweens will be more reluctant to participate in larger group activities. As an activity leader, try not to put these tweens on the spot by calling on them to answer a question or by forcing them to participate. If you have a lot of timid tweens, try running programs that involve independent work or groups of no more than two or three. On the flip side, tweens developing bodies mean they have more dexterity, making it possible to offer more advanced and detailed crafts.

Social Characteristics

The differences between younger and older tweens become more apparent in regards to their social development. While those ages ten and eleven typically stick with their own gender, twelve to fourteen year-olds are often looking for more activities that involve members of the opposite sex. As librarians, we can easily accommodate both preferences by allowing tweens to choose their own team members and their own seats for activities rather than assigning and determining these selections.

When it comes to activities, you may also notice that younger tweens are still seeking more feedback from adults, whereas older tweens crave the acceptance and support of their peers. When running programs, we always like to compliment tweens on their creations and ideas, but also give them them the opportunity to share with their peers if they so choose. For this reason, collaboration is such an important element of library programs; unless they really want to, don't make tweens work as an island unto themselves. As an activity leader, also refrain from giving assistance unless it is requested, although certainly make it clear that assistance is available if needed.

Finally, you may notice that younger tweens very much stick to the status quo, desperately trying to be like their peers in regards to dress, speech, and actions. On the other hand, older tweens may be finding ways to develop their own identity and sense of style. The best rule of thumb is to accept all tweens for who they are and who they want to be and encourage tweens to do the same.

Tweens in Libraries

Tweens are still children, not teens, when it comes to library programs, as their brains aren't "totally cognitively developed" (Kluger). Tweens are not ready for, and have less interest in, more abstract and complex teen programing. At the same time, this sophisticated demographic does not want the "baby" programs that libraries have traditionally offered to children. This is similarly echoed in the retail world, according to a recent newspaper article: A focus group of tweens suggested that "I grew up, but Crayola (products) didn't grow up with me" (Horovitz). Ten to fourteen year olds are truly in between, and thus require a unique and specialized level of service.

Over the past few years, major national retailers have realized the benefits of tapping into the tween market with exclusive make-up, accessory and clothing lines, tailor-made music, dedicated magazines and books, and so much more. Tweens want products that are made just for them (Ginsburg). They want to define their existence as separate from that of their family and as more reflective of themselves (Kluger). Tweens can define their existence within the fun and safe environment of library programs. Libraries can benefit by tapping into this niche market, too!

Why Offer Tween Programs?
- Attract new customers
- Develop lifelong library users
- Promote library collections and materials
- Promote library services
- Introduce tweens to literature
- Provide enrichment
- Provide an alternative to TV and Internet
- Help tweens understand themselves and others
- Provide a safe environment for tweens to become more independent

Resources

Ginsburg, Monica. "Serving the 'Tween' Scene." *Crain's Chicago Business* 33, no.32 (Aug 2010): 21-25.

Helmrich, Erin, and Elizabeth Schneider. *Create, Relate, and Pop @ the Library: Services and Programs for Teens & Tweens*. Neal-Schuman, 2011.

Holmes, Melisa. "Helping Your Tween Through Brain Morph". *TweenParent.com*. http://www.tweenparent.com/articles/view/278.

Horovitz, Bruce. "Tween Years Prove to Be Rewarding for Toymakers; Kids 9-12 Have Cash, and Now They Have Fun Stuff to Spend It On." *USA Today*, December 22, 2010, *http://www.usatoday.com/printedition/money/20101222/tweenstretch22_st.art.htm*.

Kluger, Jeffrey. "How to Hype-Proof Your Tween." *Good Housekeeping* 251, no.1 (Jul 2010): 85-91.

Moore, Fernanda. "Field Guide to the Common Tween," *Parenting School Years* 24, no.6 (Jul 2010): 100-103.

PUBYAC: The listserve for PUBlic librarians serving Young Adults and Children. Accessed May 1, 2011, *http://www.pubyac.org/*.

Sutherland, Anne, and Beth Thompson. *Kidfluence: Why Kids Today Mean Business*. McGraw Hill Ryerson, 2001.

Texas 4-H, and Youth Development Strengthening Clubs Initiative Team. *Ages and Stages of Youth Development*. AgriLife Extension. http://texas4h-tamu-edu.wpengine.netdna-cdn.com/files/2011/12/club_ed_training_agenda4_topic1_Ages_Stages_Presentation_Handout.pdf.

Wells, Tina. *Chasing Youth Culture and Getting it Right: How Your Business Can Profit by Tapping Today's Most Powerful Trendsetters and Tastemakers*. John Wiley & Sons, 2011.

Yarrow, Kit, and Jayne O'Donnell. *Gen BuY: How Tweens, Teens, and Twenty-Somethings Are Revolutionizing Retail*. Jossey-Bass, 2009.

Chapter 1: Get Started!

Tween Programming in Your Library

Whether you're offering tween programs for the very first time, or you're a seasoned veteran, remembering the following guidelines will make your job so much easier!

Ask the Tweens

Always consult your tween customers. Who knows better what tweens want than the ten- to fourteen-year-olds themselves! To gather this information, informally ask tweens what they would like to see offered at the library and when they would be able to attend programs (after-school, evenings, weekends). Questions can be asked either before or after a program, or even when a tween is checking out library material. Dedicated Tween Interest Groups (TWIG), as described in Chapter 10, are also an excellent avenue for discussion and brainstorming.

Tween Trends

In November 2012, we consulted numerous male and female TWIG members to find out what is trending in the world of tweens. Some of their answers were expected, while others were quite surprising and served as the perfect starting point for some fabulous new program ideas!

Trending Websites
- Facebook
- YouTube
- Twitter

Trending Video Games
- Halo 3 - A first-person shooter game set in the 26th century. Humans vs. aliens.
- Minecraft - A "sandbox" game that requires players to build, explore, combat, and create.
- Uncharted 3- Players search for a lost city in this action-adventure game.
- Wii Sports-Boxing, bowling, golf, tennis, and baseball.

Trending Television Shows
- American Idol - A singing competition.
- Love It or List It - Homeowners choose between their renovated house or a new one.
- Property Brothers - Homeowners buy a house and renovate.
- 1000 Ways to Die - The science behind different kinds of death.
- Deadliest Warrior - Historic and modern warriors battle. Think ninjas vs. zombies!
- MTV Cribs - Tours of celebrity homes.
- My Ride Rules - Car owners battle to see who has the best "ride."

Trending Movies
- Madagascar 3
- Here Comes the Boom
- Avengers
- Ice Age 4
- Meet the Fockers

Trending Apps
- Temple Run - Steal a cursed idol and run for your life!
- Doodle Jump - A jumping journey that uses jet packs, springs and more!
- Angry Birds - Use a slingshot to launch birds at various objects.
- Sim City - Build and run your own city.
- Minecraft - A "sandbox" game that requires players to build, explore, combat, and create.
- Harry Potter - Apps based on the books.
- Underwater - similar to Tetris, but underwater!

Trending Bands and Musicians
- Gangnam Style/Psy
- One Direction
- Maroon 5
- Usher
- LMFAO
- Dubstep (a genre of electronic dance music)

Surveys, both print and online, are another option to ascertain your tweens' interests. Print surveys can be made available at the library or can be mailed or taken to local schools. Online surveys can be integrated into the library website by an in-house IT department, or free online survey sites like *http://www.survey-monkey.com* can be used. Over the years, our tweens have provided us with a plethora of ideas that have succeeded in drawing more of their peers to the library. The ideas have been as simple as card and game tournaments, and as complex as scavenger hunts. Tweens want to be part of the process, so collaboration and consultation with library staff should be encouraged. In fact, some studies suggest that "middle …

school students are more likely to enroll in and stick with . . . programs if they're given lots of leadership opportunities within those programs" (Phelps Deily). You'll be surprised to see that some of your best ideas will come from the tweens themselves, who are in-touch with and drive the trends.

Look at Pop Culture

Some of our most successful programs have been inspired by pop culture. Trending right now are reality shows, video games, crafts, and anything to do with social media. Stay atop of tween trends by leafing through tween-targeted magazines like *Discovery Girls* and *J-14*.

What Are 5th - 8th Graders Reading (2011-2012)?
- Diary of a Wimpy Kid series (Jeff Kinney)
- The Hunger Games trilogy (Suzanne Collins)
- Number the Stars (Lois Lowry)
- Hatchet (Gary Paulsen)
- Percy Jackson and the Olympians series (Rick Riordan)
- The Heroes of Olympus series (Rick Riordan)
- The Outsiders (S.E. Hinton)
- The Giver (Lois Lowry)
- Frindle (Andrew Clements)
- The Tell-Tale Heart (Edgar Allan Poe)
- The Diary of Anne Frank

Source: Renaissance Learning. *What Kids Are Reading: The Book Habits of Students in American Schools.* 2013 edition. http://doc.renlearn.com/KMNet/R004101202GH426A.pdf.

SHOWING OFF THEIR FAVORITE BOOKS COURTESY OF OSHAWA PUBLIC LIBRARIES GRAPHICS DEPARTMENT

Watch general entertainment television shows like *TMZ* and more tween-centric shows on stations like Nickelodeon. Read the annual Nickelodeon Kids' Choice Award nominee and winner list to find out who is popular. Pay attention to what your tween customers are borrowing and talking about. Take a look at publishing trends for tweens (Sanderson), as these often reflect tween interests. Leaf through publishers' catalogs or speak to publisher representatives. Have your timing right and "capitalize on what's hot," (Maughan) otherwise your program might be an epic flop!

Look Online

While being a librarian in the online age can have its complications, it also has many perks, especially the ability to share and collaborate with other libraries around the world. Many librarians are posting outlines of successful and popular programs that can be adopted and adapted for your own use. It is also a good idea to subscribe to list servs such as PubYac, where library staff are posting program outlines or asking for suggestions. It is a great opportunity for networking and sharing, and is often the stepping stone for ideas of your own. Subscribing to PubYac is easy; visit *http://www.pubyac.org/subscribe.htm*, and enter your email address and a password. You will have daily digests of ideas delivered right to your inbox. You can also visit other library websites to see what tween programs they are offering. If something interests you, email the library and ask for outlines or assistance. Perhaps the biggest piece of advice we can offer is this: Don't reinvent the wheel. Most libraries work in partnership and are willing to pool creative resources.

Practice What You Know

While it's sometimes great to think outside of the box and offer completely off-the-wall programs, it is usually best to stick with what you know and with what you are most comfortable. If you try to stretch too far beyond your comfort zone, the tweens will definitely sense your anxiety. You do not need to be a pop culture whiz or try to use their lingo too much; if it fails, the tweens will just think you're lame!

It Doesn't Have to Relate to Reading

While reading, literacy, and lifelong learning are major strategic thrusts for most libraries, we can sometimes become too focused on these elements. Not every tween program needs to be a book club or based on a popular novel. There are many opportunities to showcase your collection in a more subtle way, like through book displays or scavenger hunts that require tweens to maneuver their way through the physical layout of the building. A craft program or a reality-based program is a great way to get tweens in the door to provide that stepping stone to more substantial and dedicated use of all library services.

If You Feed Them, They Will Come

Although it's been said time and time again, it is true; snacks are an important part of any tween program. Not only is it an easy way to fill a few minutes, but it is also a great way for tweens to bond with one another. Food can also act as the "icing on the cake" in creating that extra added touch that tweens will talk about and remember. There is no question that food and drink can be expensive, so you don't have to provide much. A juice box, a bottle of water, or even some candy will work. It may be a small thing, but it can have a great impact.

Swag

Attend an event or festival, and you realize how important free giveaways and promotional items are. Library programs for tweens are no different. Free prizes will leave tweens with a sense of fulfillment and enjoyment. It also gives them a piece of library "memorabilia" to take home. The swag that you offer does not need to be fancy. It can be something as simple as a pencil, or as expensive as a book or gift card. Instead of offering several small prizes, you may want to raffle one large prize, such as a video game system, event tickets, or other electronics. After each program, simply provide tweens with a ballot so they can enter their name in a drawing and leave with the anticipation that they might be the lucky winner! Giveaways can either be purchased from the library budget, or can be a donated by a local business or organization. The idea is to make tweens feel that they are getting something from and are a part of the library.

Registration versus Drop-in

Depending on your library's policies, registered or drop-in programs may be an option. Our preference is advance registration, as this affords us the opportunity to plan the number of supplies needed (our programs are usually limited to twenty participants). Advance registration also allows library staff to place reminder calls to all tweens who have registered. Tweens sometimes forget which programs they have signed up for and these calls help boost attendance. It may also be helpful to create a waiting list for programs that fill up quickly. Even if you cannot offer a space to those tweens on the designated date and time, you can keep the contact information and set-up a second program for the waiting list participants.

Days, Times, and Frequency

The day and time that you offer tween programs depends upon your local community. It is best to experiment with multiple options and ask tweens what they prefer. Based on the comments that we have received, evenings and weekend afternoons tend to work best with the tweens' schedules in our community. After-school programing for this age group has been less successful due to competition from other organizations, and because working parents are unable to drive their children to after-school programs. Most of the programs that are outlined in this book were offered on the second Monday evening of each month. If possible, maintain some consistency so tweens will know that there is always a library program on a particular day and time each month. Not only does this help to build a loyal tween following, but it also assists librarians in the planning of their busy schedules.

Resources

Discovery Girls. *Discovery Girls: A Magazine for Tween Girls. http://www.discoverygirls.com/*

J-14 Magazine. *Teen Stars - Celebrities | News | Beauty| Fashion. http://winit.j-14.com/*

Maughan, Shannon. "Betwixt and Between: How Publishers Are Reaching Out to a Vast Demographic of Eight- to Fourteen-year-olds." *Publisher's Weekly* 249, no. 45 (Nov 2002) 32-36.

Nickelodeon. *Kids Games, Kids Celebrity Video, Kids Shows. http://www.nick.com/*

Nickelodeon. *Kids' Choice Awards. http://www.nick.com/kids-choice-awards/*

Phelps Deily, Mary-Ellen. "Engaging Teens and Tweens." *Education Week* 29 no. 32 (May 2010) 5.

PUBYAC. *Subscribe/Unsubscribe. http://www.pubyac.org/subscribe.htm*

Sanderson, Caroline. "New Fashions in Non-Fiction: Is There a Gap in the Market for Accessible Non-fiction for Nine- to Fourteen-year-olds?" *The Bookseller* (Aug 2005) S8.

Survey Monkey. *Free Online Survey Software & Questionnaire Tool. http://www.surveymonkey.com/*

TMZ. *Celebrity Gossip | Entertainment News | Celebrity News. http://www.tmz.com/*

Chapter 2: Get the Word Out!

Promoting, Marketing, and Using Social Media

You can have the best library programs in the world but that means nothing if no one knows about them! To attract tweens to the library, you need to get their attention. In *The Accidental Library Marketer*, Kathy Dempsey (p. 125) says:

> *"Branding is another important aspect to consider as you look at your overall marketing picture. That's really about developing the "personality" of your product and service. How do you want people to see you? What characteristics should come to mind when people think of you?"*

Branding is the first step to promoting tween events. Something as small as what you call your program can have a huge impact on attendance. For example, by calling our poetry event Poetry Pwnage, rather than something boring like Poetry Night at the Library, we catered to gamers and the tween age group. Tween programs need their own personality that mimics that of a tween's personality – forward thinking, upbeat, pop-culture savvy, and fun! This is far different than the brand libraries already have, which is a provider of books. Of course, we love that books and libraries are synonymous, but to attract the younger crowd, we reiterate that libraries aren't just about books anymore!

Internal Marketing

Word-of-mouth is the easiest and best program promotion among tweens. Get a core group who are already library users to come to your programs. Verbally sell your programs when on the service desk or registering new tween customers. Talk about programs during in-house class visits. Try to "sell" the program as an experience rather than a product or library service. Make it sound like it's the most exciting thing tweens could possibly be doing after school during their free time, because it is!

If you have a library newsletter or calendar of events, try to create a separate section for tween happenings. Hang posters in areas of the library where tweens hang-out. Designate a bulletin board specifically for the promotion of tween-related services. This way tweens will know exactly where to look for their special events, programs, and contests.

TIFFANY PROMOTING PROGRAMS AT THE REFERENCE DESK. COURTESY OF OSHAWA PUBLIC LIBRARIES GRAPHICS DEPARTMENT

External Marketing

To further develop a core following, you can widen your audience and advertise outside the library. If you have a graphics department like our library does, ask for extra posters to display in areas where tweens normally hang out – skate parks and rinks, rec centers, movie theatres, the mall, etc.

Ask if you can have a booth or table at these locations during a busy time to talk directly with the tweens. Attend local festivals and have a presence at larger community events where library programs and services can be promoted. A great time to promote the library is when a blockbuster comes out in the movie theaters and tweens are lined up to see it--have a library booth and great give-aways!

Form a solid relationship with local public and private schools; teacher-librarians, principals, and even clerical staff can often be tremendous and powerful advocates of the public library. If local schools distribute monthly or quarterly newsletters to each student, ask if they will dedicate a small section to the promotion of public library programs. Try to get your programs advertised on the morning announcements or webpage of each school. Arrange to have a booth at schools during parent-teacher conferences and open-houses. Finally, ask if you may visit each classroom for 15 minutes or so to advertise upcoming programs; or spend a morning in the school library and have each classroom visit you. This works especially well in the months leading up to summer reading clubs and summer programming.

Teachers are also a great way to get the word out. If your library hosts class visits, always mention the upcoming tween programs, contests, and more. Show them your bulletin board, newsletter, and advertising. Hand-outs are great because tweens can take it home and show their parents. Some teachers even offer extra credit to students who attend library events on their own time - it's worth a shot! This method of advertising has certainly resulted in increased program attendance for us, and will hopefully work for you as well!

Utilize your local media. Send press releases for your larger events to local cable networks, newspapers, and radio stations. Quite often they're looking for local interest stories to highlight or community listing blurbs and libraries have a lot to offer! You might even be asked to go on local television. Press releases are simple to write and answer the: who, what, when, where, why, and how of the event. There are templates in computer editing programs and online. Below is an example of one of our press releases.

Press Release

Oshawa Public Libraries to host Battle of the Bands
We will be rocking the shelves!

The Oshawa Public Libraries is hosting a giant musical even on February 21, 2009 at the McLaughlin Branch of Oshawa Public Libraries.

There will be three categories of band playing for big prizes: Grades K-8, Grades 9-12, and adults.

Bands selected to play are:

Grades K-8:	Ponies from the Unknown Dimension	(11:00 AM)
Grades 9-12 Teen Category:	Bonafide Ride	(11:30 AM)
	Mixed Reality	(12:00 PM)
	The Nonchalants	(12:30 PM)
Adult Category:	One Divided	(2:00 PM)
	You Bet Your Life	(2:30 PM)
	Blucore	(3:00 PM)

Each category has one grand prize. Adults have the chance to compete for ten hours of free studio time at Wellcraft Music Group in Oshawa, while teens are competing for five hours studio time. K-8 contestants are competing for an exciting prize package!

Doors open to the public at 10:00 AM and admission is free! Admission is first come, first serve. Don't miss this one-of-a-kind event!

Online Event Listings

Tweens and their parents also spend a lot of time online. There are many free and popular online listings where you can post your programs:

Craigslist	LibraryThing Local	InThere.com
Kijiji	BookSaleFinder.com	Going.com
Upcoming.org	Artsopolis.com	BusyTonight.com
Eventful	YourEventHub.com	Zvents

Here are a few of the great reasons why it's important to market online:
- It is always available.
- People pass on what they read online.

- It is a friendly and conversational way to promote your programs.
- You can harness multimedia to make it fun and interactive.
- It is cheap or free.
- It is measurable – you can easily quantify if it is worth your time advertising online, as well as who came to a program after reading about it online.

Social Media

Even though they're not quite teens, tweens are definitely using social media, with Facebook (*http://www.facebook.com*) being one of the more popular sites. According to a 2012 J. Walter Thompson study of two hundred American tweens ages eight to twelve, 46 percent belonged to Facebook. Considering Facebook requires members to be at least thirteen years of age to enroll, this number is quite staggering! To reach these social media "mavens," libraries can create their own Facebook page and encourage tweens to "like" it, allowing them access to status updates, photos and more. To get more "likes," provide a link to the Facebook page on the library's main webpage, distribute bookmarks at programs, or host a contest in which tweens who like the Facebook page get their name entered in a special drawing to win a prize. If you do create a library Facebook page, be an active user and keep the page up-to-date. Ideas for status updates include advertisements about upcoming programs, new book/dvd/cd releases, questions (such as, Who is your favorite *Hunger Games* character?), and any interesting news items/trivia that tweens might like. If you receive parental permission, you can also post photos from programs so that tweens can tag themselves and have fun searching the page for their friends. And since 43 percent of the tweens in the J. Walter Thompson study feel that their real social life happens on social networks, tagging oneself and sharing the photo of a library program has huge marketing implications.

In addition to Facebook, some tweens are also joining sites like Twitter (*http://www.twitter.com*), Pinterest (*http://www.pinterest.com*), Instagram (*http://www.instagram.com*), Flickr (*http://www.flickr.com*), blogging services (*http://www.blogger.com*), and more. Incorporate these sites into library services by hosting a contest that challenges participants to create their own blog entries (book/movie reviews), or hold a Flickr photography contest.

Lastly, Youtube (*http://www.youtube.com*) has exploded in popularity amongst tweens, as they search for viral videos to watch, share, and comment on. To keep up with this trend, many libraries are now creating a YouTube channel where promotional videos can be uploaded. Video ideas include clips of library programs and events, program advertisements, and booktalks. YouTube video contests are also extremely popular now that most tweens have video capabilities on their mobile and hand-held devices. Ask tweens to make their own video (which should either be filmed in the library or at the very least mention the library) and email the link to you. Submissions can then be screened and uploaded to the library YouTube channel.

The world of social media is always changing and varies regionally. What's hot one minute can be definitely not the next. With the rise in popularity of smart phones, apps like SnapChat, SongPop, CandyCrush, Vine, Plants vs. Zombies, and more come and go seasonally. It's hard to keep your finger on the social media pulse but well worthwhile if you are looking at cutting-edge ways to reach out to tweens.

If you make it fun, they will come!

Create fun and different names for the programs, poll the tweens about what they'd like to do, use popular culture as a compass, and you'll never go wrong planning for tweens. If you have a healthy publicity and programming budget, consider getting promotional items that are out of the ordinary, such as: lip balm, nail files, microwavable popcorn, stress balls, lanyards, and more. This way you have something with your library's logo on it to give away as prizes – great advertising!

Resources

Christopher, Martin, Adrian Payne, and David Ballantyne. *Relationship Marketing: Bringing Quality, Customer Service and Marketing Together*. Butterworth- Heinemann, 1991.

Coote, Helen. *How to Market Your Library Service Effectively* (2nd ed). Aslib, 1998.

Dempsey, Kathy. *The Accidental Library Marketer.* Information Today, 2009.

Gronroos, Christian. *Service Management and Marketing: Managing the Moments of Truth in Service Competition*. Lexington, KY: Lexington Books, pp. 128-9. 1990.

Gupta, Dinesh K. "Marketing in Library and Information Context: Myths and Realities." *Library Science* (now SREL *Journal of Information Management*)35(2) June, 1998. pp. 99104.

Gupta, Dinesh K., and Ashok Jambhekar. "Developing a Customer-Focus Approach to Marketing of Library and Information Services." *Desidoc Bulletin of Information Technology* 22(3) May, 514. 2002.

Hart, Keith. *Putting Marketing Into Action*. London: Library Association Publications Ltd. 1999.

Hayes, H. Michael. "Another Chance for the Marketing Concept." In *The Art and Management of Business Management*, vol.7: Marketing, edited by Dale A. Dimpe. New Delhi: Jaico, pp. 273-87. 1995.

Kenneway, Melinda, "Marketing the library" Presentation delivered at UKSG Annual Conference, April, 2007. Retrieved from *http://www.tbicommunications.com/UKSG07.pdf*

Koontz, Christie. "Stores and Libraries: Both Serve Customers." *Marketing Library Services* 16(1); Jan/Feb. *http://www.mls.com*. 2002.

Lovelock, Christopher H. *Services Marketing* (2nd ed.). Prentice Hall, 1991. pp. 2234.

Orava, Hilkka, "Marketing Is an Attitude of Mind." Proceedings of the 63rd IFLA General Conference, August 31September 5, 1997. *http://www.E:\IFLA\IV\IFLA63\63ARRM.HTM*.

Palley, Will. *Gen Z: Digital in their DNA*. J. Walter Thompson Company. *http://www.jwtintelligence.com/wp-content/uploads/2012/04/F_INTERNAL_Gen_Z_0418122.pdf*

Rajagopal. *Marketing Management: Text and Cases*. Viklas, 2000. pp. 56.

Weingand, Darlene. *Future-Driven Marketing*. American Library Association, 1998.

Chapter 3: Get the Party Started!

Icebreakers

Since tweens crave security and acceptance (Wells, p.57), it is a good idea to start each program with an icebreaker or a "get to know you" activity. This is especially important if you are hosting one-time programs for which different participants register each time. During each program, it is also essential to focus on interaction among the participants through the use of group activities. Even if some activities better lend themselves to independent work, there is always the opportunity for interaction through the sharing of ideas. Ask tweens to share with the group what they are working on, or how they are executing their projects. Not only does this keep the atmosphere light, but it also allows for new friendships to be formed. Below are our favorite icebreakers. Additional icebreakers can be found online by visiting the links listed in the resources section.

Acrostic Name Poem

Each tween writes his/her first name vertically down the left side of a piece of paper. S/he must then think of a word that describes him/her for each letter. After everyone is done, each tween shares with the group.

Candy Introductions

American chef and food writer James Beard said that "food is our common ground," so let's get to know another person through food. Have a bowl of various colored candy, such as M&Ms or Skittles, available as tweens arrive for the program. Ask each person to take a few candies and they can eat all but one. Each color of candy represents a different question, such as: "Red is What is your favorite subject at school?" "Green is How many siblings do you have?" "Yellow is What is your favorite place in the world?" "Brown is What are your career ambitions?" "Blue is What is your favorite book?" List the colors and corresponding questions on a piece of chart paper. Once everyone has arrived, reveal the chart and have tweens answer the matching question as they introduce themselves to the group.

I Never . . .

Arrange chairs in a circle, one for each tween, minus one. Choose one person to be "It," who will stand in the center of the circle. "It" names something s/he has never done (e.g. "I have never... been water skiing"). Anyone who *has* done the thing that was mentioned has to get out of his/her chair and find another empty chair to sit on. They may not sit in the same seat. Whoever is "It" tries to grab one of the empty chairs during the chaos. The person who is left without a chair becomes "It" and must stand in the middle of the circle. S/he then states something they have never done and tries to get a chair. If a person has been in the center of the circle at least three times and can't think of anything they've never done, they can yell, "Train wreck!" Everyone has to move on this one.

Line-up

The object of this icebreaker is to have tweens line-up according to their birthdays (months and days only). Sounds easy right?! Well, the catch is that no one is allowed to speak while trying to arrange themselves! Instead of birthdays, you might try alphabetically by first or last name.

Name Your Favorite

This one is easy! Ask tweens to state their names and their favorite game show, book, or movie character, food, vacation destination, superhero, Greek god/goddess, or whatever the theme of the program might be.

New Friends Bingo

As they enter the program, give each tween a new friends bingo card. Once everyone arrives, tweens can partner with someone they do not know. The partners color in each square if they share the attribute in that square. The first duo to form a line can call "bingo" to win a prize. Another version is to have tweens mingle and color in a square if they meet someone with one of the listed attributes.

NEW FRIENDS

BINGO

B	I	N	G	O
Has the same birth month as you	Chooses Winter as their favorite season	Has a favorite food that is anything other than pizza	Was extremely nervous about starting a new school year	Read 5 or more books during the summer
Has the same favorite school subject as you	Bought more school clothes than usual	Has a sibling	Woke up before the alarm went off this morning	Did not ride the bus to school today
Gets up before 6:00 a.m. on school days	Brought their lunch to school today		Has the same favorite color as you	Traveled out of state this summer
Has the same number of siblings as you	Has more than one pet	Lives close enough to walk to school	Participated on a team this summer	Shares the same eye color with you
Is excited to be back in school	Has lived in the same house for their entire life	Picked out their clothes before the first day of school	Brought a snack to school today	Plays a musical instrument

Choose a person you do not know well. Create a list of things you have in common.

String Game

Place a ball of string or yarn and a pair of scissors in the middle of a circle of tweens, and have each tween cut a piece. They may choose how short or long the string will be. Once everyone has cut a length, they take turns telling the group about themselves while wrapping the string around their pinkies. Those who have cut long strings will have quite a bit of talking to do, while those who have cut shorter lengths will be able to keep it short and sweet! You may wish to cut the string prior to the program so that lengths are a reasonable size, and the tweens can each choose one.

True or False

True or False is an icebreaker that can be used to fit many different themes and it also requires tweens to use the library collection to do some research. Library staff may wish to pull relevant books ahead of time, or may ask the tweens to find the books for their statements. Tweens will use the books to craft statements about the program topic. Some of these statements should be true, and some should be false. Each tween reads a statement to the group and the participants must guess whether the statement is true or false.

Two Truths and a Lie

Ask each tween to come up with three statements about themselves. Two must be true and one must be a lie. After mixing up the order, tweens can read their statements to the group and participants must guess which of the statements is a lie. Sometimes it's easier for tweens if they can write their statements down on paper. This way the lie is less obvious!

Urban Legends

While this icebreaker is specific to the Urban Legends program found in Chapter 13, it can also be used at any program as a fun introduction. Explain that an Urban Legend is a modern folktale or stories that may or may not be true. Ask tweens to tell their own urban legend or scary story. You may also wish to use the urban legends found at *https://sites.google.com/site/thetweenscene/,* and read them to the group, asking tweens to guess if they are real or legend.

Would You Rather

One of the most requested icebreakers is "Would You Rather?" In this game, library staff presents tweens with two options, both being unusual, gross, or weird. Tweens must then state which of the two options they prefer. One example is, "Would you rather see someone trip and fall, or see someone start dancing out of nowhere?" Rather than reading questions to tweens, it is sometimes more fun to type questions on slips of paper for tweens to randomly select and read aloud. This is a game that gets everyone talking! For "Would you rather" questions, visit *http://www.rrrather.com/,* or purchase a copy of *Would You Rather...?*

For Kids! by Justin Heimberg and David Gomberg, Seven Footer Press, 2007. Note that there are multiple editions in the *Would You Rather* series, and the title for kids would be most appropriate for tweens.

Resources

Eslflow. *Icebreakers to Inspire Communication.* *http://www.eslflow.com/ICEBREAKERSreal.html*

Icebreakers.WS. *Icebreaker Games Collection.* *http://www.icebreakers.ws/*

Knox, Grahame. *40 Icebreakers for Small Groups.* *http://insight.typepad.co.uk/40_icebreakers_for_ small_groups.pdf*

The Source for Youth Ministries. *Games and Icebreakers.* *http://www.thesource4ym.com/games/default.aspx?Search=Mixers*

The Ultimate Camp Resource. *Ice Breakers.* *http://www.ultimatecampresource.com/site/camp-activities/ice-breakers.html*

Wells, Tina. *Chasing Youth Culture and Getting it Right: How Your Business Can Profit by Tapping Today's Most Powerful Trendsetters and Tastemakers.* John Wiley & Sons, 2011.

Chapter 4: January

It may be cold outside in January, but the library is heating up with scavenger hunts, trivia games, New Year's parties, and everyone's favorite sweet: chocolate! Two of January's programs are spin-offs of popular television shows, while another program focuses on food, which is popular with growing tweens. The final program allows tweens to ring in the New Year, Beijing style, with a fun-filled Chinese New Year Party! The big question is this: Who will have more fun – the tweens or the library staff members running the program?

The Amazing Race: Library Edition

From coast to coast and from continent to continent, facing detours, U-turns, roadblocks, and pit stops, many teams have competed to make it to the final leg of CBS's reality show, *The Amazing Race*. And now, local tweens have the opportunity to compete with this library-friendly version. This cost-effective program will take tweens on a wild ride through the library, as they work in pairs to find clues, complete challenges, and learn about the world around them.

Program Advertisement

Get your passport ready as we play the library version of *The Amazing Race*! Participate in road blocks and detours by completing some puzzling and crazy challenges.

Number of Spaces Available

A maximum of 30 spaces.

Program Preparation (3 hours)

1. Re-write the following clues to reflect your collection, space, and needs. Our version is also available online at *https://sites.google.com/site/thetweenscene/*.

    First clue: Where will you be headed to first? A popular destination for New Year's Eve, this city is home to the Greenest Lady in the world. While you're here, be careful not to drop the ball on the Big Apple! Where are you headed? Let your travel agents know.

    Answer for library staff only: New York City

    Finding aids: State atlases, books about various states

    Second clue: ROAD BLOCK: Now that you are in the Big Apple, you have to get to the capital city of Brazil. You can't fly into the capital city if you don't know what it's called. Find the answer in a book and let your travel agents know when you have the right answer!
    Answer for library staff only: Brasilia
    Finding aids: Books about Brazil

    Third Clue: DETOUR: Work or Play? You are on your way to Ancient Egypt (bet you didn't know we could time travel!), but first you must find information on WORK or PLAY. Research an ancient occupation or sport: For WORK: Write down the job title and tell us if you would enjoy this job. For PLAY: Find a book about games in ancient Egypt, tell us if you would like to play.

    Finding aids: Books about Ancient Egypt

    Fourth Clue: ROAD BLOCK: You're headed to Antarctica (the auditorium). A family of penguins needs your help! You must transport their eggs from their old nest to their new nest.

    Materials needed: beach balls, which tweens must place between their knees and transport from one side of the room to the other.

    Fifth Clue: PIT STOP: Good job helping those penguins! Now it's time for a short pit stop in Australia, where you will eat a meal with the natives of this country. Your travel agent will direct you to your next destination.

    Materials needed: Dirt Cups (see recipe below) and a travel video about Australia

    Sixth Clue: DETOUR: Speak it or See it? Welcome to China! You must now decide if you want to SPEAK IT or SEE IT. SPEAK IT: Say hello in Mandarin Chinese to your travel agents. SEE IT: Find a photo of a Chinese tourist destination, show your travel agents the picture.

    Answer for library staff only: Nî hâo (informal) / Nín hâo (formal) / Nîmen hâo (plural)

    Finding aids: Books about China

Seventh Clue: FAST FORWARD: Since it takes forever to travel over the Russian Steppes, you need to fast forward by finding a brochure or document with your library's logo. Take it to your travel agent to get your next clue.

Eighth Clue: ROAD BLOCK: You're in England, and you've been invited to tea with the Queen, but you do not have a thing to wear! Make a fancy outfit using the supplies in the auditorium. One of you will be the model, the other is a designer. You have five minutes to complete this challenge and get your next clue.

    Materials needed: Clothing and toilet paper

Ninth Clue: FAST FORWARD: You must cross the Atlantic Ocean to get back home. Before you board the ocean liner, make sure you're not sailing on the date that the Titanic sunk! The answer lies in an encyclopedia. The first team to give their answer to the travel agent wins!

    Answer: April 15, 1912

    Finding aid: Encyclopedia

2. Print clues and the Amazing Race: Library Edition Travel Journal so that tweens can make notes (15 copies each)

3. Prepare Pudding Dirt Cups (15 minutes). This dirt dessert recipe is a great cooking activity for tweens. Made with chocolate pudding, crushed Oreos or other cookie, and gummy worms, these pudding dirt cups are as fun for the kids to make, as they are tasty to eat. This recipe makes about 10 servings.

    Ingredients:

    - 8-10 pudding cups or you can make your own pudding ahead. Get chocolate and vanilla pudding cups.
    - 8 oz. frozen whipped topping (such as Cool Whip), thawed
    - 1-1/2 cups crushed sandwich cookies (such as Oreos), or you can buy the box of crushed cookies.
    - 20-30 gummy worms, spiders, whatever gummy insect you prefer.

    Preparation: Combine pudding cups with frozen whipped topping and ½ cup of crushed cookies. Put in the fridge for about 5 minutes to thicken. Spoon into as many cups as you need (recipe will make about 10-15 cups). Sprinkle remaining crushed cookies on each cup over the pudding mixture. Top each cup with 2-3 gummy worms. Chill in the fridge until you are ready to serve! There are many Dirt Cup recipe variations online.

4. Hide the clues in the appropriate places.

5. Make sure all library staff members know that the race is happening and should not remove any program materials.

The Amazing Race: Library Edition Travel Journal

Use this journal to record any information that you need to bring back to your travel guides.

_____

_____

_____

_____

_____

_____

_____

_____

_____

_____

_____

_____

_____

_____

_____

_____

_____

_____

_____

_____

Room Set-Up

5 tables and chairs for snacks

1 table to register tweens as they enter the program

Set-up DVD player and television/projector

An open space for the costume contest and penguin activity

Pull books on the various states, China, and Brazil and place them throughout the library with the next clue. This will make it easier for younger tweens to keep pace during the race.

You may wish to leave the books about Ancient Egypt and the encyclopedias on the shelves.

Program Outline

1. Icebreaker: Ask tweens to state their names, and what their favorite vacation destinations would be.

2. Formation of teams: Divide tweens into groups of two. If there are uneven numbers, there may be a team of three.

3. Review the following rules:

    • Clearly state acceptable and prohibited areas. (ie. Clues will only be found in the teen area. Entering the quiet study area is prohibited.)

    • No running.

    • No disruptive behaviour.

    • Wait in line for your turn.

    • Read your clue card and carefully follow directions.

4. The Race is On! The First Leg: Teams can now be given their first clue card, as well as a travel journal to record any information. Tweens should work their way through the corresponding activities.

5. Pit-Stop: Mid-way through the program, tweens enjoy a pit-stop in Australia where they eat a wormy dirt cup (Australian Aboriginal People often eat insects found in the ground) and watch a travel video. Not only does this pit-stop give tweens a needed break, but it also allows lagging teams to catch up, evening out the playing field.

6. The Race is On! The Second Leg: After the pit-stop is over, tweens venture back into the library to complete the race.

7. Record the names of the winning team, as well as the order that the remaining contestants finish.

8. Award prizes: Books are a great prize for this program. It is sometimes nice to give all participants a prize. The winning team chooses first.

9. Clean up.

Materials Used

- Toilet paper and other articles of clothing for the costume contest
- Beach balls for the penguin activity
- A travel video for the pit-stop
- DVD player and television/projector
- Chocolate pudding cups, sandwich cookie crumble, worm-shaped chewy fruit snacks, and plastic spoons and cups for the dirt cups
- Juice and water for the pit-stop
- Books about the various states (especially New York), Ancient Egypt, China, Brazil, and encyclopedias
- Travel journals and clue cards
- Pencils

Budget

Approximately $50 was spent on food and juice.

General Comments

If you have a lot of younger tweens in your group, they may have trouble finding the answers to all of the clues. That's why pulling books and putting them in a more prominent area will help to ease frustration. Even with the books pulled, tweens had a difficult time deciding which pile belonged to which clue. This program was definitely a hit with tweens frantically racing to find the next clue. Many tweens suggested we run a second race so that they could compete once again. Detailed information about *The Amazing Race* television show is available online at Wikipedia: *http://en.wikipedia.org/wiki/The_Amazing_Race*

Are You as Smart as a 5th Grader?

Appearing at the top of the Nielsen ratings in 2007 and 2008, and more recently, turned into a popular Nintendo Wii® video game, Fox's *Are You Smarter Than a 5th Grader* still airs nightly and is watched by many tweens and their families. With the combination of adult and tween players, and easy and difficult questions, this trivia game appeals to all ages and will definitely be a hit at your library! While the creation of trivia questions can take some time, this is ultimately a very cost effective program, and it is also very easy to run. All you need are some eager fifth or sixth grade students and some brave adults to compete against them! With minimal set-up and equipment, this program can also be easily transported to local schools for family literacy nights or class visits.

RACING AROUND THE LIBRARY DURING "THE AMAZING RACE: LIBRARY EDITION." COURTESY OF OSHAWA PUBLIC LIBRARIES GRAPHICS DEPARTMENT.

Program Advertisement

Did you just finish fifth grade in June? Do you remember what you learned in social studies, math, science, and other subjects? If so, you are eligible to play the library's version of the popular TV game show, *Are You Smarter Than a Fifth Grader?*! Compete against the adults of (insert your community's name) to show them how smart fifth graders really are! Competition spaces are limited. To register for the competition, please call (insert phone number). Audience members can register for free at any branch.

Number of Spaces Available

5-10 tweens, unlimited audience members; the number that appear on-stage depends upon the length of each game, the length of the program, and the number of games you create.

Program Preparation (5 hours)

1. Familiarize yourself with the state curriculum, including content/subject areas and core learning goals (laws of motion, land masses, etc.) for each grade. You should be able to find full curriculum guides for your state online.

2. Each game will consist of two first, second, third, and fourth grade questions respectively, as well as three fifth grade questions, one of which will be used for the $1,000,000 question.

3. For each game, randomly assign a subject area to each grade level. For example, the first game may have the following categories:

    -   First Grade Social Studies, First Grade Health
    -   Second Grade Math, Second Grade Science
    -   Third Grade Social Studies, Third Grade Health
    -   Fourth Grade English Language Arts, Fourth Grade Math
    -   Fifth Grade World Languages, Fifth Grade Health, Fifth Grade Social Studies (as the $1,000,000 category)

4. Write the questions for each category. To help with the workload, you may want to assign each staff member a subject area. S/he will then be responsible for all of the questions in that area, regardless of the grade level. Use the state curriculum as a guideline, and use books and the Internet to come up with questions. The following sample questions are taken from a variety of state curriculum guidelines.

    First Grade Social Studies
    -   What are the four cardinal directions?
    -   Answer: north, south, east, west

First Grade Health

- True or False: Hand washing is a good way to prevent the spread of germs.
- Answer: true

Second Grade Math

- What is 200-175?
- Answer: 25

Second Grade Science

- What is the brightest object in the sky?
- Answer: the sun

Third Grade Social Studies

- On which continent is the United States located?
- Answer: North America

Third Grade Health

- Which of the following is a positive action towards another human or towards an animal? A) anger B) respect C) rudeness
- Answer: B) respect

Fourth Grade English Language Arts

- Happy is a _____ for joyful. A) synonym B) antonym C) homonym
- Answer: A) synonym

Fourth Grade Math

- The fraction 7/10 could be written as the decimal _____.
- Answer: 0.7

Fifth Grade World Languages

- "La casa" is the Spanish word for what?
- Answer: house/home

Fifth Grade Health

- What is the system responsible for taking in oxygen and removing carbon dioxide from the body? A) Circulatory B) Respiratory C) Excretory D) Digestive
- Answer: B) respiratory

Fifth Grade Social Studies ($1,000,000 category)

- What are the three branches of United States government?
- Answer: Executive, Legislative, Judicial

5. Once all of the questions have been developed, input them into a Microsoft® PowerPoint presentation or attach them to cue cards if you are using a physical, low-tech version of the game. A digital presentation is available online at *http://point4teachers.com/5ᵗʰ%20Grader.htm*

6. Test the game to make sure that it works correctly and to ensure that you know how gameplay works. Check for spelling and grammatical errors! More detailed information about gameplay is available online at Wikipedia: *http://en.wikipedia.org/wiki/Are_You_Smarter_Than_a_5ᵗʰ_Grader%3F*.

Room Set-up

2 tables with 5 chairs around each at the front of the room for the fifth or sixth grade students

Place blank slips of paper and pencils at each space, or use dry erase boards and markers.

Place a number of chairs in the middle and back of the room for the audience members.

At the front of the room, set-up a computer and projector, and a microphone (optional), as well as a table for prizes.

You may also want a podium at the front of the room for contestants to stand behind.

Program Outline

1. As audience members arrive, write each contestant's name on a piece of paper and place it in a hat or container. As fifth and sixth graders arrive, assign each student a seat at the front of the room and attach a name card to the table in front of them.

2. Introduce the fifth and sixth graders, including name, grade, which school they attend, and any favorite subjects/hobbies/career aspirations, etc. The tweens will love being the center of attention, and this will also give contestants a good idea of each tween's academic strengths.

3. Explain the rules: Explain how the game is played, including "peeks," "copies," and "saves" (see below).

4. Game One:
    -   Randomly select a name from the hat or container to play the first game. Ask the contestant to introduce him or herself, including profession, hobbies, etc.
    -   That lucky contestant will step up to the podium, or designated game play area, and choose a preferred grade and subject area, such as First Grade Social Studies.
    -   The library staff member running the PowerPoint presentation will click on that button, revealing the question.
    -   While the contestant is thinking of the answer, each fifth and sixth grader will write down his or her answer.
    -   The contestant has several options when answering the question:
        -   Provide the answer if they think they know it.
        -   Choose to "peek" at a fifth or sixth grader's answer (once the peek is used the contestant may answer the question with the answer of his or her choice). A "peek" can only be used once per game and the contestant may randomly choose to "peek" at any tween's paper.

- Choose to "copy" a fifth or sixth grader's answer (this automatically locks in the fifth or sixth grader's answer as their own). A "copy" can only be used once per game and the contestant may randomly choose to "copy" any tween's paper.

- Once the contestant has provided an answer, the library staff member will click anywhere on the slide to reveal the correct answer, then click on the slide again to return to the main gameplay screen.

- If the contestant gets the answer correct, click on the $1000 money designation slot on the far left of the screen. Continue until all questions have been answered correctly, until the contestant "drops out/quits," or until the contestant "flunks out/incorrectly answers a question."

- If the contestant gave an incorrect answer, he or she has one chance to "save" themselves by choosing to look at any one fifth or sixth grader's answer. If that answer is correct, the contestant moves on to the next round. If that answer is incorrect, the contestant "flunks out" and the game ends. A "save" may only be used once per game.

- Hand-out prizes as suitable.

5. Remaining games: Continue with new contestants until time or games run out!

6. Clean up.

Materials Used

- Computer and projector
- Screen
- Microsoft® PowerPoint presentation or physical gameboard
- Microphone (optional)
- Slips of papers and pencils or dry erase boards and markers for tweens to record their answers
- Prizes
- Hat or container
- Paper and tape for tween name tags

Budget

The budget for this program is quite minimal. The only expense will be prizes for participating audience members, as well as a small gift for each participating tween. Prize suggestions include books, gift cards, or library promotional items such as mugs, pencils, and magnets.

General Comments

Depending on which time of year you run this program, you can invite fifth grade or sixth grade students to participate. We initially ran the program in September and invited sixth graders who had just finished the fifth grade in June. If you run the program too early in the school year, the fifth graders will be at a disadvantage to answer fifth grade questions, as they will likely not have covered that material at school yet. Registration for this program can also be tricky, as there are two sets of participants – tweens who will appear "on stage," and then everyone else who wants to compete as an audience member. If you pre-register for your programs, be sure to clarify this with participants as they sign-up. To cut corners when writing questions, you may want to purchase the board game version of *Are You Smarter Than a 5th Grader*, which is available in most retail outlets or online. Just note that the relevancy of questions and level of difficulty will vary dependent upon the state in which you live. To play this game with an all-ages audience or at a family literacy night, simply eliminate the tween players and either play as a group, or ask one person to be brave and choose a category. If they do not know the answer, call on the entire group to help out.

Chocolate, Chocolate Everywhere

With its rich history and world-wide appeal, you can't go wrong with a chocolate-themed program, especially in the middle of a long and dark winter! As with most food-based programs, this one will draw large crowds to the library. In fact, we have had lengthy waiting lists and have offered the program multiple times in multiple locations to satisfy the tweens' need for chocolate! This is also a very versatile program that can take on many different titles, including Chocolate Olympics, Make Your Own Chocolates, Taste Tests, and more! There are more activities included in this outline than you will have time for in one program, so pick and choose those that you like best.

Program Advertisement

Calling all chocolate lovers! Make and decorate your own molded chocolates and gift box; dip into our chocolate fondue; win exciting treats with chocolate trivia; and vote for your favorite chocolate bar! Kick off the New Year with tons of chocolate!

OR

Calling all chocolate lovers! This is your chance to try many kinds of chocolate and vote for your favorite! There will be games, prizes, and of course – chocolate!

Number of Spaces Available

Due to the costs associated with this program, as well as the sugar-induced hyperactivity level of the tweens, a maximum of 15 spaces is recommended.

Preparation Time (2-3 hours)

30 minutes to melt the chocolate, if you are using fondue or making molds, and to chop up chocolate bars for the taste test. If you don't have chocolate making supplies, add shopping time. Molds and melting chocolate can be purchased at most large craft stores.

Program Preparation

1. Copy the following passing game story.

The Creamy Chronicle of Chocolate

Let's go back in time, about 4000 years ago to be exact, for this is when the people of Mexico and Central America first discovered that beans growing on the cacao (kah kow) tree could be used to create the tasty treat we call chocolate!

The Mayans and Aztecs were among the first to roast and grind the cacao bean into a powder. But they didn't use this powder to make chocolate bars. Instead they mixed it with water to create a bitter chocolate drink, to which they often added cornmeal and chili peppers. For the Mayans, this chocolate drink symbolized life and was used in numerous religious and marriage ceremonies. In Aztec culture, cacao beans were a symbol of wealth and were often used as currency. Only the priests, merchants and Aztec nobility could afford to drink chocolate.

Chocolate wasn't introduced to Europe until after the Spanish explorers invaded the Americas in the 1500's. Explorers like Christopher Columbus and Hernan Cortez didn't necessarily want the cacao beans to create chocolate though. Instead they wanted to use the beans as currency. It didn't take long for the people of Spain to fall in love with the taste of chocolate, especially after they discovered that adding sugar and milk made it a much sweeter treat, similar to the hot chocolate that we drink today. Soon, most of Europe was obsessed with this exotic and delicious new beverage!

IMAGE 4.2 COURTESY OF OSHAWA PUBLIC LIBRARIES GRAPHICS DEPARTMENT.

There weren't any major changes in the production of chocolate until the Industrial Revolution in the late 1700's; around the same time that chocolate was introduced to North America. The invention of the cocoa press made the beans easier to process, reducing the price and making it available to a wider audience. Finally, in the 1800's, solid chocolate was made for the first time, leading to the creation of the chocolate bar as we know it today.

There is a lot of debate surrounding the nutritional value of chocolate. Many researchers are now finding several health benefits when the right kind of chocolate is eaten in moderation. For example, did you know that dark chocolate, which contains more cocoa and less sugar, can actually help fight tooth decay? Or that eating chocolate will not significantly raise your cholesterol level? Or that dark chocolate is good for your cardiovascular health? Dark chocolate has also been linked to improved blood flow to the brain and can help to lower stress levels. Chocolate also contains super high levels of the chemical phenylethylamin, which makes people very HAPPY. So next time someone offers you a piece of chocolate, take a bite and enjoy!

Print the following trivia questions.

True or False

Cocoa beans were once used as currency.	TRUE
Chocolate is nutritious.	TRUE (to an extent)
M & Ms were first created for the U.S. Military.	TRUE (wouldn't melt)
Baking chocolate contains no milk solids or sweeteners.	TRUE
Switzerland produces the most chocolate.	FALSE (USA)

Multiple Choice

Which is better for you?

A. Milk Chocolate B. *Dark Chocolate* C. White Chocolate

Which area of the world produces the most cocoa?

A. South Asia B. *West Africa* C. South America

The word chocolate is derived from what language?

A. French B. Latin C. *Mayan*

In 1657 the first chocolate shop opened in…

A. *London* B. Vienna C. Barcelona

The Swiss top the scales with most chocolate consumption per year. How many pounds of chocolate does the average Swiss person eat per year?

A. 2 lb. (907 g) B. 10 lb. (4.5 kg) C. *22 lb. (10 kg)*

3. Write point values on pieces of paper for the trivia game.

4. Print instructions for paper gift boxes available online at *http://www.homemade-gifts-made-easy.com/free-gift-box-templates.html,* and *http://www.homemadegiftguru.com/origami-box-instructions.html.*

5. Chop up each chocolate bar and place a small piece on a spoon (15 of each chocolate bar variety). Using a marker, write the corresponding number on the top of the spoon.

6. Cut up slips of paper for voting.

Room Set-up

3-4 tables, depending on activities

1 table to register tweens as they enter the program, and also to display relevant books from the collection

A microwave for melting chocolate

Program Outline

1. Icebreaker: Ask each tween to introduce themselves and to tell the group their favorite kind of chocolate.

2. Chocolate Passing Game: In this game, a library staff member will read the chocolate passing game story. Each time the word "chocolate" is said, tweens must pass the box of chocolates they are holding. At the end of the story, the person holding the box of chocolates is the winner.

3. Chocolate Trivia: This is a chance for tweens to test their knowledge of chocolate history and trivia using the questions and answer slips.

4. Chocolate Moulding: This is where things start to get really messy, but really fun! There are a great variety of candy and chocolate molds for purchase at dollar stores, craft stores, and even online. Select molds that are tween-friendly, like musical instruments, stars, sports, flowers, etc. It's easiest to melt the chocolate in the microwave in a plastic sandwich bag, and then cut the tip of the corner of the bag. This will make it easier to squeeze the chocolate into the molds. Once tweens have filled their molds, place them on a baking sheet and set them in the freezer to set until the end of the program. You may wish to purchase several colors of melting chips to paint the molds before filling, as well as flavoring oil and sucker sticks. For more information visit *http://www.ehow.com/how_4477905_make-chocolate-molds.html*

5. Gift Boxes: Once the chocolate is poured, tweens can make their own gift boxes. For samples and templates of two homemade paper gift boxes, see *http://www.homemade-gifts-made-easy.com/free-gift-box-templates.html* and *http://www.homemadegiftguru.com/origami-box-instructions.html*.

6. Chocolate Relay Race: In this two team relay race, tweens wear a pair of oven mitts, run to a table, pick up a Hershey Kiss®, unwrap it, and run back to their team. The oven mitts are transferred to the next person in line and the race starts again! The race is over once each team member has had a turn. The team to finish first receives a prize!

7. Chocolate Bar Taste Test: Now's the time for tweens to actually start eating chocolate and to vote for their favorite. Assign each brand of chocolate bar a number and record it on a sheet of paper for safe keeping. Tweens can sample each bar and write the number of their favorite on a slip of blank paper. A library staff member can tally the votes and reveal the winner.

8. Chocolate Fondue: Everyone loves a fondue party, including tweens! In a fondue pot, melt a *lot* of chocolate. Tweens can take turns dipping a variety of items into the pot: pretzels, fruit, cookies, potato chips, and marshmallows. Have plates and lots of napkins on hand.

Materials Used

- Many different kinds of chocolate, including chocolate bars, Hershey Kisses®, a box of chocolates, and chocolate melting chips. Be aware of nut allergies when buying chocolate.
- Chocolate or candy molds
- Sucker sticks

- Flavoring oils, if desired
- Microwave
- Plastic sandwich bags
- Oven mitts for the chocolate relay
- Knife and spoons for the chocolate taste test
- Slips of paper and pencils for chocolate bar taste test votes
- Tablecloths
- Fondue pot
- Plates, napkins, and fondue sticks
- Pretzels, fruit, cookies, potato chips, and marshmallows for dipping
- Paper and scissors for gift boxes

Budget

Depending on the quality of chocolate you buy and the number of activities you offer, this program can cost $20 to $200.

General Comments

This is a fun and exciting program. In order for it to run smoothly, arrange for volunteers to help with clean-up and to transfer the molds to the freezer. Because the tweens will get very excited and hyper, it helps to firmly set ground rules at the beginning of the program, then have fun. This is a great program to offer in a typically low attendance month, as it is sure to boost your statistics!

Chinese New Year Party

Tweens (and people of all ages) continually seek the opportunity to learn about the various cultures and customs that make the world such an interesting place. The library is the perfect venue for opening doors to a whole new experience where tweens can immerse themselves in the traditions and celebrations of a nation. And January/February is the perfect time to explore the customs of China, as this is when Chinese New Year is celebrated! Since Chinese New Year marks the beginning of a new lunar year in the Chinese calendar, the date changes each year, but celebrations always take place in either January or February. Consult an online calendar to verify the date each year. Chinese New Year is sometimes also referred to as the Spring Festival or Lunar New Year celebration. Whatever you call this program, it is sure to be a hit with tweens as they learn about the symbols and traditions of Chinese New Year through a variety of craft and activity stations. So have fun, and Gung Hay Fat Choy (Happy New Year)!

Program Advertisement

_____(insert date) marks the Year of the _____ (insert Chinese zodiac symbol) on the Chinese Lunar Calendar. Celebrate the Chinese New Year holiday with great food, activities, crafts, and more. For tweens ages 10-14.

Number of Spaces Available

30

Program Preparation (3hours)

1. Contact local Chinese food restaurants to negotiate a deal on Chinese food.

2. Print the Chinese zodiac table of dates and the Chinese zodiac character trait hand-outs.

3. Pull books from the collection that contain Chinese symbols and their meanings. Or, find a variety of symbols online and print them out for tweens to use.

4. Find crafts and activities related to specific zodiac animals (if required).

5. Print copies of the Chinese New Year word search and trivia questions.

6. Using any word processing or graphics program, design a bingo sheet for each tween. Shuffle the images on each card.

Room Set-up

Tables and chairs for the various stations, preferably one for each

An open area for bingo

Program Outline

1. Icebreaker: Chinese zodiac match-up. Give each tween a copy of the zodiac table of dates so they can find their Chinese zodiac sign based on their date of birth. Ask all "like" signs to group together. You may have to group two signs together if tweens can't find another person with the same sign. Distribute the Chinese zodiac character trait handout. Ask tweens to discuss whether or not these descriptions are accurate of their sign.

2. Paper Lanterns: Lanterns are such an important part of the Chinese New Year that a lantern festival is held on the fifteenth day to celebrate the sighting of the first full moon. In order to bring about

Year of the...
2013: Snake
2014: Horse
2015: Goat/Sheep
2016: Monkey
2017: Rooster
2018: Dog
2019: Pig

Ideas for bingo card images:
- Chopsticks
- Cow/Ox
- Dog
- Dragon
- Dumplings
- Fireworks
- Flag (Chinese)
- Flower
- Fortune Cookie
- Great Wall of China
- Goat/Sheep
- Horse
- Karate
- Lanterns
- Map of China
- Monkey
- Panda
- Pig
- Rabbit
- Rat
- Red envelope
- Rooster
- Snake
- Tiger

Chinese Zodiac

To find out which zodiac animal you are, find your year of birth below……

1996	February 18	to	1995	January 31	Pig
1997	February 6	to	1996	February 19	Rat
1998	January 27	to	1997	February 7	Ox
1999	February 15	to	1998	January 28	Tiger
2000	February 4	to	1999	February 16	Rabbit
2001	January 23	to	2000	February 5	Dragon
2002	February 11	to	2001	January 24	Snake
2003	January 31	to	2002	February 12	Horse
2004	January 21	to	2003	February 1	Goat
2005	February 8	to	2004	January 22	Monkey
2006	January 28	to	2005	February 9	Rooster
2007	February 17	to	2006	January 29	Dog
2008	February 6	to	2007	February 18	Pig
2009	January 25	to	2008	February 7	Rat
2010	February 13	to	2009	January 26	Ox
2011	February 2	to	2010	February 14	Tiger

The Chinese Zodiac

If you were born in the year of the Rat, you are intelligent and quick to take advantage of any opportunity. You are hardworking, efficient, organized, practical and innovative. You thrive on challenges and are very handy to have around in times of crisis. A fun-loving person, you're right at home at parties and other social events. You enjoy the company of others, but also value your privacy. On the negative side, you run the risk of being selfish or stubborn. You can also be anxious.

As a person born in the year of the Ox, you are calm, dependable, steady, logical, and methodical. You respect traditions and dislike taking risks. You are somewhat of an introvert and need peace and quiet to do your work. As a friend, you are truthful, honest, fair-minded, patient and sincere. While the ability to stick to your decisions is admirable, you need to be careful that you don't become stubborn or inflexible. On rare occasions, you may also lose your temper.

Those of you born in the year of the Tiger often seem larger than life. You are excited by a challenge and throw yourself wholeheartedly into everything you do. Powerful, daring, colourful, rebellious, exciting, courageous, optimistic and determined, you are a natural leader. Negative traits include a big ego, stubbornness, and self-centeredness when you don't get your way. Perhaps your worst fault is that you will do anything to get revenge if you've been crossed!

The Rabbit is the symbol of a long life. Therefore, people born in the year of the Rabbit are considered very fortunate. You are charming, elegant, gracious, kind, and generous. With your reserved nature, you are happiest in a peaceful environment. You have no interest in being in the spotlight and work hard at avoiding confrontations. You have good judgement and tend to be lucky with money. On the other hand, you can often be too cautious and may lose out on promising opportunities. You also have a tendency to put yourself first.

With your majestic personality, it's probably easy for people to identify you as someone born in the year of the Dragon. A bit of a show-off, you love being the center of attention. Your boundless energy and enthusiasm for life make you an exciting person to be around. You are generous, loyal, open with your feelings and quick to forgive. You are a natural leader. On the negative side, you may feel that you are better than others and may be too demanding of others.

People born in the year of the Snake are difficult to figure out. A secretive person, you treasure your privacy and rarely show your true feelings. You seem to have been born with a certain wisdom and you trust your own instincts. Graceful, elegant, well-mannered, and soft spoken, you're attracted to the nice things in life. You are the deepest thinker of the signs. Your fabulous sense of humour can make anyone laugh. You like having power in your hands. However, you are sometimes willing to do anything to succeed. You can also be very demanding of others.

Independent, unpredictable, and adventurous are some words that describe those born in the year of the Horse. Everything about you is quick, from your physical movements to your speech. Others confide in you because you are genuinely interested in them. You are cheerful, honest, and warm. You are good at handling money and may be wealthy. However, your changeable nature can cause difficulties for you and your friends. You may neglect to finish one thing before moving on to something else. You can also be hot-tempered.

If you were born in the year of the Goat, you are a gentle, sensitive and dreamy person. You go out of your way to avoid conflict and are distressed if you hurt someone or let them down. An emotional person, you are moved by things of beauty, such as a painting or piece of music. You have artistic talent. You have a peaceful nature and kind heart. You dislike schedules and do not like being disciplined. Competition, pressure, and unexpected situations throw you for a loop. You can have difficulty making decisions.

Clever, inventive, and quick-witted, the Monkey is the most ingenious of the Chinese cycle. A remarkably quick study, you're able to solve difficult problems with ease. There is nothing you can't do if you put your mind to it! You are charming and persuasive and extremely social. You are spontaneous, humorous and are willing to work hard. On the negative side, you are not a very trusting person and can be jealous of other people's success.

If you were born in the year of the Rooster, people can't help but notice you. You love being the center of attention and work hard to get there. Cheerful, amusing, witty, and intelligent, you're a born performer. You are also a perfectionist and a hard worker. However, you can often be too honest in criticizing people to the point of hurting their feelings. Even though you appear to be confident, underneath you may not be that confident after all.

The Dog is the symbol of justice and those born in the year of the Dog are always ready to fight for a worthy cause or to defend those being unfairly treated. You are honest, intelligent, straightforward and deeply loyal to your friends. You have the ability to see people for who they really are. You are open-minded and want to know all of the facts before making a decision. You have few negative traits—you may lack patience and have a tendency to snap at people who irritate you.

As someone born in the year of the Pig, you are innocent and very trusting. You hate fighting and see no reason why everyone can't get along. You are an honest, generous, kind and understanding person. You enjoy social gatherings and parties. You are hardworking, but have little interest in being in charge. Your main downfall is that you are too trusting of others who may take advantage of your kindness.

Chinese New Year's Word Search!

```
I I R L A N T E R N F E S T I V A L R W
N S S A P M O C A U B P A V A D N A P S
G R N G N I T N I R P R E G N I F Z G A
A E E I S E L D O O N D N A E C I R E G
I F T P N O A U Q F U P U P E G E S F P
B O I H A L Y Z N M K L E L K A E J T M
N R U R J P N S P A J B E L T N P J A L
S T T N E X P L A Y R B I W I R E S R R
I U C C G W I J N U R S A H N F X N E E
N N B G D N O O L A C L C S C N A R H Z
H E D M G O O R T J L E Q H I T E E T G
V C R S M M Y I K O G E C Q E A F T F N
I O U D W R O O F S N O G A R D N N O I
N O C E S N O C A L E N D A R Z U A R J
C K N C X B H T I U R F E E H C Y L A I
Q I A Z M I E G H A P P I N E S S F E E
R E E A N E W Y E A R Z S T R Y B C Y B
D S B A M B O O S H O O T S S K T I G Y
E V D W P W S O P G H P U O R E G G G D
L O N F O R S E L C Y C N O O M A G N Y
```

ASIA	DRAGONS	LYCHEEFRUIT
BAMBOO	DUMPLINGS	MOONCYCLES
BAMBOOSHOOTS	FINGERPRINTING	NEWMOON
BEANCURD	FIREWORKS	NEWYEAR
BEIJING	FORTUNECOOKIES	PANDA
CALENDAR	GREATWALLOFCHINA	PAPER
CELEBRATION	HAPPINESS	RICEANDNOODLES
CHINA	LANTERNFESTIVAL	SILK
CHINESE	LANTERNS	SOYSAUCE
COMPASS	LUNARSCHEDULE	YEAROFTHERAT

Chinese New Year Trivia

1. What is the name of the Calendar where New Year's Day is January 1st?
    a. Julian Calendar
    b. Gregorian Calendar
    c. Jewish Calendar
    d. Chinese Calendar
2. What calendar determines the date of the Chinese New Year?
    a. Lunar
    b. Solar
    c. Chinese
    d. Zen
3. At the turn of the Millennium (year 2000) what was the year according to the Chinese New Year?
    a. Horse
    b. Rabbit
    c. Dragon
    d. Snake
4. What is the Chinese Zodiac for the year 2012?
    a. Rat
    b. Snake
    c. Dragon
    d. Tiger
5. How long does the celebration of Chinese New Year last?
    a. 1 day
    b. 10 days
    c. 14 days
    d. 15 Days
6. Often red envelopes are passed out during Chinese New Year. What is in the envelopes?
    a. Money
    b. Candy
    c. Firecrackers
    d. Beads
7. What colour are the paper lanterns during Chinese New Year?
    a. Red
    b. Blue
    c. Green
    d. Yellow
8. The red envelopes are usually exchanged between whom?
    a. Elder to younger
    b. Man to woman
    c. Woman to man
    d. Brother to sister

Answer Key:
1b, 2a, 3c, 4c, 5d, 6a, 7a, 8a

a cheerful environment, Chinese people gather and hold their lanterns up to the sky. Tweens can make their own paper lanterns by folding a piece of rectangular paper in half lengthwise to create a long rectangle. Draw a 1 inch line on the non-folded side of the paper. Next, draw lines that are 1 inch apart, going from the folded edge to the line just drawn. Cut these lines. Unfold the paper and decorate one side using markers, stickers and foam pieces. Using tape or glue, attach the edges together so a lantern is formed. Add a handle and string multiple lanterns together for full effect!

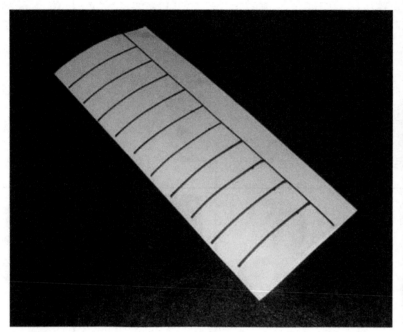

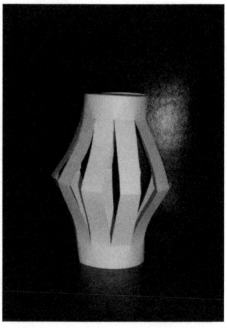

PHOTO CREDIT: BRIANNE WILKINS-BESTER   PHOTO CREDIT: BRIANNE WILKINS-BESTER

3. Chinese New Year Fan: Folding fans have been used for centuries in China as a story-telling tool and most often as part of Chinese dance performances. Folding fans are easy to make. Using a paintbrush and black paint, draw a variety of Chinese symbols onto three pieces of construction paper. Once dry, fold each paper accordion style, and glue the three pieces together. Wrap a pipe cleaner around the base of the fan to form a handle. Since red is a lucky color in Chinese tradition, consider using red paper.

4. Red Envelopes: Giving someone a red envelope filled with money or a lucky coin is an important Chinese New Year tradition. Tweens can make their own red envelopes by using templates found online. For an easy to make envelope, try *http://www.activityvillage.co.uk/red_envelope_template. PDF*. For a more elaborate template, visit *http://todaysnest.typepad.com/todays-nest/2012/01/chinese-new-year-the-red-envelope.html*.

5. Chinese Zodiac Animal Crafts: In addition to general Chinese New Year crafts, you might also include crafts and activities specific to the zodiac symbols. So, in 2014, you could search the internet or your files for a horse-themed craft.

6. Worksheets and Trivia: Include a worksheet station for tweens who finish their crafts early.

7. Chinese New Year Bingo: As the program winds down, gather everyone together for a few rounds of bingo. Instead of calling "Bingo," have tweens yell "Gung Hay Fat Choy" when they have a winning line. Use books, library promotional items, and bookmarks as prizes.

8. Snacks: Try partnering with a local Chinese food restaurant so that you can serve some traditional Chinese fare. If you are serving food, make sure an allergy alert notice is included in program advertising. A lot of Chinese food can contain MSG, shellfish and nut oils.

9. Clean up.

Materials Used

- Colored construction or regular paper
- Scissors
- Markers
- Rulers
- Stickers
- Foam pieces
- Glue
- Tape
- String
- Pipe cleaners
- Paintbrushes
- Black paint
- Bingo card chips
- Prizes
- Chinese food

Budget

Approximately $40-$60 depending on how many you have coming out or if you have food available.

General Comments

The popularity of this program never seems to dwindle. As a result, it has been offered several times, each time drawing just as large a crowd! In addition to tweens, a large number of adults and kids wanted to attend as well. Because self-directed stations and simple crafts are budget friendly, this program was eventually opened to people of all ages, including tweens. If you have a group of tweens who are exceptionally crafty, consider purchasing Chinese New Year craft kits online or through a catalog. Oriental Trading (*www.orientaltrading.com*) has an excellent offering, including prizes and decoration ideas.

Chapter 5: February

It's February, the month of love! William M. Thackeray once said, "To love and win is the best thing," and we couldn't agree more. This is definitely a winning month at the library with some exciting programs designed to woo tweens through your doors. The first program celebrates a love of delicious cupcakes, and the second, a love of a timeless and classic game show. For those tweens who have yet to find love or are a little more cynical, there is a celebration of un-love with the Anti-Valentine's Day Party, a program sure to draw lots of media attention to your library! To promote and spread the love between friends and classmates, we also have an Anti-bullying friendship bracelet program to share.

CILF: Cupcake I'd Like to Frost

Everyone loves a cupcake! There are television shows and numerous cookbooks devoted to this petite dessert because they are cute and fun and make everyone happy. One hurdle may be that you are not a baker or cake decorator and do not feel comfortable hosting a program like this. That's why we decided to bring in a professional. We contacted a local bakery to see if they'd host a class and bring the cupcakes. They were more than happy to oblige and were also very reasonable in price. This program is an example of looking at what is popular in the world around you and adapting it to be tween and library friendly.

Program Advertisement

Discover the fun of decorating cupcakes! Your instructor will show you the right way to decorate, step by step. Supplies will be provided. Registration is limited.

Number of Spaces Available

15 (this will vary depending on your materials)

Program Preparation (30 minutes)

1. Contact local cake decorator to arrange a workshop.

2. If you choose to run this program on your own, purchase supplies and practice techniques.

3. Pull cake decorating books from the collection to display during the program.

Room Set-up

Tables and chairs for 15

Program Outline

Start with a simple icebreaker: The tweens introduce themselves and say their favorite flavor cupcake. Then, they start decorating! Our instructor taught the four basic ways of piping on the frosting, how to make basic flowers, and how to make a cupcake look like a cute little creature.

Materials Used

This will depend on if you are leading this program yourself or if you are bringing in a professional. If you are buying all the decorating materials, a good place for one-stop shopping is a craft store like Michael's.

Budget

We spent $100 on the instructor and materials. It was a flat rate and the instructor brought everything with him.

General Comments

You may find our title for this program too cheeky for your community. Try Cupcake Warz, Cupcake Party, Decorate a Sweet Treat, Cupcake Mania, If You Give a Tween a Cupcake, or simply, Decorate a Cupcake.

PLAYING GAMES BEFORE CUPCAKE DECORATING. COURTESY OF OSHAWA PUBLIC LIBRARIES GRAPHICS DEPARTMENT

Is the Price Right?

Everyone loves a good game show, especially one that is based on the long-running and popular American television series, *The Price Is Right*, hosted by Bob Barker and more recently, Drew Carey. In this program, tweens will use their knowledge of prices to bid on actual hardcover or paperback books that the library has secured as prizes. If the tweens have a good sense of the price, they will go on to compete in more fabulous pricing games! Luckily, unlike the television version, libraries do not actually have to purchase the big ticket prizes, but can instead display product images on flip-chart paper or Microsoft ®PowerPoint slides. While this program does involve a fair bit of preparation, it is a very cost-effective choice that nicely incorporates literacy through the use of books as the items up for bid. Once the initial preparation is complete, the program can be recycled and re-used at a later date or at another library branch.

Program Advertisement

Come on down, you're the next contestant! Test your skills and knowledge at this game-show themed program. Win prizes!

Number of Spaces Available

20 (however 12-16 would be ideal to ensure that all contestants get a chance to play)

Program Preparation (5 hours)

1. Obtain 20 books (less if fewer participants) to be used as prizes and items up for bid. Write a short book talk for each title.

2. Purchase or create a prize wheel.

3. Purchase candy to be used as additional prizes.

4. Choose up to 20 games to be played. It is important that you are comfortable with and have a basic knowledge of the games that are being played. Because some of the games require extensive props, it is key to choose those that are appropriate to your library's budget, space, and use of staff time. In most instances, games can be played using a combination of Microsoft® PowerPoint presentations and paper flip charts.

THE PRICE RIGHT? PRIZE WHEEL.

THE PRICE RIGHT? ONE AWAY FLIP CHART GAME

5. Select products to be used with the games above. When choosing retail items to showcase, consult local sale papers and store websites to obtain the actual retail price. Product suggestions include video games, snacks and beverages, clothing and apparel, and sporting goods.

6. Using new products and games, re-create a digital copy of the presentation, which is available online at *https://sites.google.com/site/thetweenscene/*. Flip charts may also be used.

Room Set-up

Tables and chairs for contestant row

Chairs for audience members

Flip chart, projector, and screen at the front of the room

Program Outline

1. Registration: As participants arrive write each contestants name on a piece of paper and place it in a hat or container.

2. Icebreaker: Choose any icebreaker from Chapter 3.

3. The First Item Up for Bid

   - Randomly select four names from the hat or container to "Come on down!" to contestant row.

   - Booktalk the first book.

   - Ask all contestants to write their bids on paper.

   - Contestants simultaneously reveal their bids.

   - The contestant with the closest bid, without exceeding the actual retail price of the book, is the winner of the book and becomes the first on-stage contestant.

   - If all contestants have over-bid, a re-bidding must occur.

4. The First Pricing Game

   - The lucky winning contestant is invited to the stage to play the first game.

   - After the contestant has played his or her game, s/he may take some candy and sit in the audience to assist other contestants with their bids.

5. Subsequent Bids and Pricing Games: Repeat step three, but select only one name to fill the vacant spot. Next, repeat step four.

6. The First Spin-off: Repeat steps three and four until approximately half of the contestants have played. At this point, it is time for the first spin-off. Both spin-offs can be played using either a purchased or home-made game wheel. Home-made wheels can be as complex as a three dimensional wooden structure or as simple as pieces of paper pinned together with a paper fastener. Regardless of the type of wheel you choose, it should contain various coin denominations, including a $1 section. Each contestant who has appeared on stage should spin the wheel, trying to attain a total of $1 in one or two spins. In each of the two spin-offs, the contestant who spins closest to $1, without going over, will progress to the showcase showdown. In the event of a tie, another spin-off will be necessary.

7. Subsequent Bids and Pricing Games: After the first spin-off is complete, repeat steps one and two until all contestants have played or until the program is in the remaining ten minutes. At one point, there may only be one person in contestant row.

8. The Final Spin-off—See step 6.

9. The Showcase Showdown: The two contestants who won the spin-offs will now compete in the coveted showcase showdown! To play this final game, select six to eight large ticket items that

Some games that can be easily adapted to a library environment include:

- Dice Game
- Hi-Low
- Lucky $even
- Most Expensive
- One Away
- Pick-A-Number
- Squeeze Play
- Swap Meet
- Switch?

An extensive list of all game ideas are available online at Wikipedia: *http://en.wikipedia.org/wiki/List_of_The_Price_Is_Right_pricing_games*.

will appeal to tweens. Suggestions include video game systems, computers and hand-held devices, electronics, bicycles, skateboards, cars, and even all-inclusive vacations. Display each item on a separate Microsoft® PowerPoint slide, grouping the items into two separate showcases. Research the actual price of these items using sale papers or websites, and record prices on a separate sheet of paper. Reveal the first showcase and ask the first contestant for their bid. Next, reveal the second showcase and ask the second contestant for their bid. The contestant who has bid closest to the actual amount without going over wins.

10.   Clean up.

Materials Used

- Flip chart
- Markers
- 2 dice
- Computer and projector
- Screen
- Microphone (optional)
- Microsoft® PowerPoint presentation
- Sales papers
- Prize wheel
- 20 books to be booktalked
- Candy
- Hat or container
- Scrap pieces of paper
- Pencils or pens

Budget

The budget for this program can vary greatly, depending on whether you purchase or make your own prize wheel. If prize books can be purchased using the book budget, or can be secured through donations, the cost can remain minimal.

General Comments

Not only did the tweens enjoy placing their bids, but the library staff enjoyed listening to their answers. It is very interesting to see how much value tweens actually assign to specific items. You'll be surprised by how off the mark, or sometimes, how accurate they really are! While it is not necessary for all tweens to compete in the pricing games, it is nice if attendance is small enough to allow everyone the opportunity to play. We love this game and wouldn't want to miss the chance to play!

Anti-Valentine's Day Party

Valentine's Day is the obvious event to plan programming around in February. This can get tricky because the aspect of love excites some tweens and others are still grossed out by any notion of romance. What should we do for those of us who hate the lovey-dovey aspect of Valentine's Day? Un-celebrate it, of course! Tweens love the dark aspect of this idea, and there is room to be as creative as you wish. Be prepared for greater attendance than you normally get at programs, at least that seems to be the experience of those libraries who try this program. Everyone can channel his or her angsty side, while making fun of this holiday and celebrating friendship. This party can be as big or small as you'd like it to be, selecting from the following events, as needed. At our library, the teen advisory board hosts Anti-Valentine's Day, which guarantees participants. We also ask the teen advisory board what kind of stations and events they think would be cool at this event. Adapted to your time and budget, this can be a great idea for your library.

Program Advertisement

Love stinks! Tweens can un-celebrate Valentine's Day with cranky crafts, moody music, and spiteful snacks. Participants are encouraged to wear black and red to the party. Help plan this event at the January 6 Teen Advisory Board meeting.

Number of Spaces Available

30

Program Preparation (3-4 hours)

1. Cut five hearts out of paper for each tween.

2. Print copies of the celebrity couple quiz and romance novel covers.

3. Print a list of famous couples.

4. Gather sock puppet supplies.

5. Fill the piñata.

Room Set-up

Tables and chairs for the various stations, preferably one for each

A circle of chairs in the middle of the room for the icebreaker

Program Outline

1. Anti-Conversation Hearts: At the beginning of the program, each tween designs five anti-conversation hearts. During the party, anyone caught saying: heart, Valentine, love, hug, or kiss has to give a heart to the person who caught them. The person with the most hearts receives a cheesy Valentine gift. Tweens can help themselves to Valentine's themed snacks throughout the program.

2. Icebreaker: Play the "I Never" icebreaker found in Chapter 3.

3. Break-Up Letter Contest: Tweens break into teams of three and work on a break-up letter. The letter will be judged on humor, originality, and mastery of writing. The judges--either the librarian or the tweens themselves--pick winning the letter and that team wins a prize – the cheesier the better!

4. Celebrity Couple Quiz: We created a quiz called "What celebrity couples are still together?" It's fun to look up the different celebs and find out who's together and who's not. Make sure you don't use one from a previous year because more than likely your answer key will be wrong!

5. Make Your Own Voodoo Dolls or Gothic Sock Puppet (also known as Gocks): For this activity we set out socks, stuffing, eyes, fabric markers, feathers, etc. and let the tweens create their own puppets or dolls in any fashion they chose. Visit the online site *http://www. ehow.com/how_4510419_make-goth-sock-puppet.html* for more information.

6. Vandalize a Romance Novel Cover: This one is easy! Either raid your romance novel collection and make copies of the covers, print out book covers from the Internet, or use your discards. Tweens write the funniest things on these covers.

7. Heartbreakers List: Have the tweens make lists of "The Top 10 Worst Places to Break Up," "The Top 10 Worst Places to Have a Date," and "The Top 10 Worst Valentine's Day Presents.

8. Word Search

9. Find My Match Game: Tape a name, one of a famous couple, to each tween's forehead or back. They have to find their match by asking questions. Use famous couples through history, celebrity couples, or even literary couples.

Are These Celebrity Couples Together or Not?
- Angelina Jolie and Brad Pitt
- Kat Von D and Jesse James
- Selena Gomez and Justin Bieber
- Vanessa Hudgens and Zac Efron
- Katy Perry and Russell Brand
- Demi Moore and Ashton Kutcher
- Kate and William
- Sarah Michelle Gellar and Freddie Prinze Jr.
- Kristen Stewart and Robert Pattinson
- Taylor Swift and Taylor Lautner
- Miley Cyrus and Liam Hemsworth
- Scarlett Johansson and Ryan Reynolds
- Mila Kunis and Macaulay Culkin
- Ashlee Simpson and Pete Wentz
- Rachel Bilson and Hayden Christenson

Anti-Valentines

```
I T L O R T N O C D R U Y S A R
U I O A E A I P D B I T T E R U
U S N O I T C E F F A S I D S O
A R L D E C T R E J E A L O U S
D A E C I C O U Y H O E I I R E
U E Y M E F N S G A T Y T B K A
N T R J E N F A I B P A S R E E
H O E R T A O E Y T R O O R E H
A R C E W V N L R O N O H L E B
P N K V I O D P A E N A K A R E
P U A E S I P S E D N N R E S A
Y P L N T D E I F S I T A S N U
K K L G E A A D L P L K C A L B
E C R E D N H I C E U A P K N E
U I I A A C V L S P S T I N K S
I S S B D E S S E R P E D H E T
```

ANNOYANCE
BITTER
BLACK
ANTISOCIAL
BREAKUP
BROKEN
DARK
DESPISE
DISAFFECTION
DISLIKE
DISPLEASURE
EVIL
HATE
HEARTLESS
HOSTILITY
LOATHE
LONLEY
REJECTED
REVENGE
SAD
SOUR
STINKS
UNHAPPY
JEALOUS
CRY
CONTROL
MEAN
TORNUP
SICK
ALONE
TEARS
TWISTED
INDIFFERENT
DEPRESSED
UNSATISFIED
AVOIDANCE

Can You Match Up These Famous Lovelorn Couples?

Iseult	A. Romeo
Cathy	B. Cupid
Rose DeWitt Bukater	C. Kevin Federline
Psyche	D. Tristan
Helen of Troy	E. Lancelot
Britney Spears	F. Heathcliff
Guinevere	G. Jack Dawson
Juliet	H. Odyssus
Penelope	J. Paris

9. Break the Piñata: We try to find the cheesiest Valentine's Day piñata possible. You can even make your own piñata if you have the time! Visit *http://www.ehow.com/how_8322567_make-heart-pinata.html* to learn how.

10. Clean up.

Materials Used

- Color copies of romance novel covers
- Printouts of broken hearts, Heartbreakers lists, quizzes
- Pencils
- Markers
- Tape
- Lots and lots of food and candy (Valentines and non-Valentines food)
- Pipe cleaners
- Googly eyes
- Socks
- Feathers
- Fabric markers
- Glue
- Piñata
- Valentine's Day related prizes

Budget

Approximately $60

General Comments

This was a very popular program for us! The teens from the teen advisory board put on the program for the tweens and everyone had a great time. It's interesting to see how angsty the kids can really get! Every year it gains quite a bit of media attention. To see past media coverage of our event, check out Carola Vyhnak's article in "Singles Unite to Say Nay to Cupid's Day" in the Toronto Star at *http://www.thestar.com/news/gta/article/760186--singles-unite-to-say-nay-to-cupid-s-day* and Stefanie Swinson's article in Durham Region News "Oshawa Teens Celebrate Anti-Valentine's Day" at *http://www.durhamregion.com/news/article/1133508--oshawa-teens-celebrate-anti-valentine-s-day.*

Anti-Bullying Bracelets

In Canada, we have an event called *Pink Shirt Day* which is an anti-bullying event that occurs the last Wednesday in February. On this day, students and participants are asked to wear a pink shirt in solidarity to symbolize a stand against bullying. You can visit *http://www.pinkshirtday.ca/* for more information. This does not take place in the United States, but different school districts host their own similar events.

Program Advertisement

In awareness of *Pink Shirt Day* on February 27, and to show your commitment to a bully-free lifestyle, make an anti-bullying bracelet. Express yourself and wear your bracelet proudly. Share them with friends, and spread the word - bullying stops here!

Number of Spaces Available

20-25 (this will vary depending on your materials)

Program Preparation (30 minutes)

1. Research different styles of friendship bracelets and decide what you'd like to offer.

2. Practice techniques and decide if you'd also like to host a conversation on bullying or show any YouTube video that has an anti-bullying message.

3, Purchase or gather materials.

4. Pull any books on friendship or anti-bullying. See sidebar for list of suggestions.

Room Set-up

Tables and chairs for 20-25

Program Outline

If you don't mind being too serious, you could start by having the tweens introduce themselves and talk about a time that they were either bullied, a bully, or a bystander and how it made them feel. If that's too much for you to handle, you can always try one of our icebreakers listed in Chapter 3. Then you can describe the different bracelets that they can make and ask tweens if they have any styles that they prefer.

Materials Used

- embroidery floss, a variety of colors
- safety pins
- any additions you'd like: beads, pop-can tabs, etc.

Budget

We already had the floss on hand, but you may have to purchase it. You can also purchase the kits from stores like Michael's for about $20.00 - $30.00 each.

General Comments

Research and practice what kind of bracelets you'd like to make! Don't be surprised if some tweens know many different types and if others have never done it before. Facilitate discussion about bullying, listen, and promote a safe and happy atmosphere.

Try these books about friends!
- *The Sisterhood of the Travelling Pants* Series by Ann Brashares
- *The End of Everything* by Megan Abbott
- *The Outsiders* by S.E. Hinton
- *When You Reach Me* by Rebecca Stead
- *Pedro and Me: Friendship, Loss, and What I Learned* by Judd Winick
- *The Perks of Being a Wallflower* by Stephen Chbosky
- *Paper Towns* by John Green
- *The Future of Us* by Jay Asher
- *Give Up the Ghost* by Megan Crewe
- *The Boy in the Striped Pajamas* by John Boyne

Chevron Friendship Bracelet

Step 1
Cut 1 strand of each color to desired length. For this particular pattern, 50 inches will produce approximately a 5 inch (including loop and knot) tight bracelet.

Step 2
Fold strands in half and make a loop and knot at the top. Pin the knot to your workstation pillow.

Step 3
Arrange colors: 12345 54321. The outer strands (blue) will be used first.

Step 4a
Knotting a row:
Starting on the right and using the outer-most strand, make four **backward-backward knots**, one on each strand in from the right, until you reach the middle. So you know 1BB on the red, 1BB on the yellow, 1BB on the green, and 1BB on the brown. You've done half of one row.

Step 4b
From the left with the outermost-strand, (in the picture, this would be the blue on the left) make five **forward-forward knots**. 1BB on the left red, 1BB on the yellow, 1BB on the green, 1BB on the brown, and the 5th BB knots onto the other blue strand. This fifth knot joins the blue strands together. They which should both now be in the center. The color arrangement will be 23451 15432.

Step 5
Your next left most and right most strand is red. Continue steps 4a and 4b until you reach the desired bracelet length.
The picture below shows what it looks like after knotting the brown row.

Step 6
Finishing: Divide the strands into two sections, and braid each group.

You're Done!

The **Backwards Knot** starts on the right and moves left.

Lay the right thread (yellow) on top of the left (red).

Loop the right thread under the left and pull upwards.

Then do it again. ** Very very important!! You need to do this twice or your bracelet will curl!!!

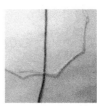 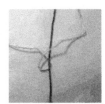

For the **Forwards Knot**, start with the thread on the left (red).

Lay the thread on top of the right thread (white). This should make the number "4".

Loop the left thread (red) under the right thread (white) and pull upwards.
Then do it again .

** Very very important!! You need to do this twice or your bracelet will curl!!!

Each F-Knot is a double half-hitch knot. You must repeat this little loopy knot twice. One time is a half-hitch (a.k.a. HH) , twice is a forward knot.

The left thread will now be on the right.

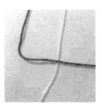 

Chapter 6: March

March signifies that spring is on its way. In Canada, it also brings March Break which is one of the busiest weeks of the year at public libraries across the nation. Spring break in the U.S. often falls in March, too, and it's always smart to have programming for tweens who are looking forward to having something to do instead of sitting around the house – or getting into trouble. Here are three tried-and-true programs to try: Library Iron Chef, A Wee Bit of Fun, Ukrainian Egg Decorating and 80s Party.

Library Iron Chef

If we could pick one single thing that brings tweens to the library, it might be the promise of food! Any program that that revolves around food is a program with a full house. Based on the popular television series, *Iron Chef*, Library Iron Chef starts with tweens crafting a chef hat and naming their team. Each team creates and names culinary delights in three categories: appetizer, main course, and dessert. The tweens judge each other's dishes and vote for their favorites! Your job is coming up with the mystery ingredient.

PLAYING NINTENDO WII DURING MARCH BREAK. COURTESY OF OSHAWA PUBLIC LIBRARIES GRAPHICS DEPARTMENT.

Program Advertisement

Do you have what it takes to earn the title of Library Iron Chef? Then this competition is for you! Come and show off your culinary skills, but beware the mystery ingredient!

Number of Spaces Available

20 (depending on your food budget)

Program Preparation (2-3 hours)

1. Determine what the mystery ingredient will be. Chocolate or marshmallows are great suggestions.

2. Decide which additional food products will be available for the chefs to use.

3. Print copies of all judging sheets.

APPETIZER

Please judge on creativity, presentation, taste and best use of mystery food.

My favorite Appetizer belongs to team:

_____

** You cannot vote for your own appetizer**

APPETIZER

Please judge on creativity, presentation, taste and best use of mystery food.

My favorite Appetizer belongs to team:

_____

** You cannot vote for your own appetizer**

APPETIZER

Please judge on creativity, presentation, taste and best use of mystery food.

My favorite Appetizer belongs to team:

_____

** You cannot vote for your own appetizer**

APPETIZER

Please judge on creativity, presentation, taste and best use of mystery food.

My favorite Appetizer belongs to team:

_____

** You cannot vote for your own appetizer**

APPETIZER

Please judge on creativity, presentation, taste and best use of mystery food.

My favorite Appetizer belongs to team:

_____

** You cannot vote for your own appetizer**

APPETIZER

Please judge on creativity, presentation, taste and best use of mystery food.

My favorite Appetizer belongs to team:

_____

** You cannot vote for your own appetizer**

APPETIZER

Please judge on creativity, presentation, taste and best use of mystery food.

My favorite Appetizer belongs to team:

_____

** You cannot vote for your own appetizer**

APPETIZER

Please judge on creativity, presentation, taste and best use of mystery food.

My favorite Appetizer belongs to team:

_____

** You cannot vote for your own appetizer**

MAIN COURSE

Please judge on creativity, presentation, taste and best use of mystery food.

My favorite Main Course belongs to team:

_____

** You cannot vote for your own main course**

MAIN COURSE

Please judge on creativity, presentation, taste and best use of mystery food.

My favorite Main Course belongs to team:

_____

** You cannot vote for your own main course**

MAIN COURSE

Please judge on creativity, presentation, taste and best use of mystery food.

My favorite Main Course belongs to team:

_____

** You cannot vote for your own main course**

MAIN COURSE

Please judge on creativity, presentation, taste and best use of mystery food.

My favorite Main Course belongs to team:

_____

** You cannot vote for your own main course**

MAIN COURSE

Please judge on creativity, presentation, taste and best use of mystery food.

My favorite Main Course belongs to team:

_____

** You cannot vote for your own main course**

MAIN COURSE

Please judge on creativity, presentation, taste and best use of mystery food.

My favorite Main Course belongs to team:

_____

** You cannot vote for your own main course**

MAIN COURSE

Please judge on creativity, presentation, taste and best use of mystery food.

My favorite Main Course belongs to team:

_____

** You cannot vote for your own main course**

MAIN COURSE

Please judge on creativity, presentation, taste and best use of mystery food.

My favorite Main Course belongs to team:

_____

** You cannot vote for your own main course**

DESSERT

Please judge on creativity, presentation, taste and best use of mystery food.

My favorite Dessert belongs to team:

_____

** You cannot vote for your own dessert**

DESSERT

Please judge on creativity, presentation, taste and best use of mystery food.

My favorite Dessert belongs to team:

_____

** You cannot vote for your own dessert**

DESSERT

Please judge on creativity, presentation, taste and best use of mystery food.

My favorite Dessert belongs to team:

_____

** You cannot vote for your own dessert**

DESSERT

Please judge on creativity, presentation, taste and best use of mystery food.

My favorite Dessert belongs to team:

_____

** You cannot vote for your own dessert**

DESSERT

Please judge on creativity, presentation, taste and best use of mystery food.

My favorite Dessert belongs to team:

_____

** You cannot vote for your own dessert**

DESSERT

Please judge on creativity, presentation, taste and best use of mystery food.

My favorite Dessert belongs to team:

_____

** You cannot vote for your own dessert**

DESSERT

Please judge on creativity, presentation, taste and best use of mystery food.

My favorite Dessert belongs to team:

_____

** You cannot vote for your own dessert**

DESSERT

Please judge on creativity, presentation, taste and best use of mystery food.

My favorite Dessert belongs to team:

_____

** You cannot vote for your own dessert**

Room Set-Up

5 tables for teams to work on

1 table for food

1 table or cart for microwave

Program Outline

1. Form Teams: Assign tweens to a team as they arrive (5 teams of 4 works well).

2. Icebreaker: Each team decides on a team name and writes it on a piece of cardstock for their table.

3. Craft: Create a chef hat using tissue paper and poster board.

4. Go over the following rules:

   - No running.

   - No disruptive behavior.

   - One person per team at the food table at any one time.

   - One person per team at the microwave at any one time.

   - Only one microwavable bowl and plate may be used per team.

   - Each course must include the secret ingredient.

   - Teams cannot vote for their own creations.

   - No finger licking or sampling until voting time!

5. The Event

   - Reveal food items that are available for use, including the mystery ingredient.

   - Discuss any potential food allergies.

   - Teams have 1 hour to create and name an appetizer, main course, and dessert.

   - Each team has the opportunity to describe their completed dishes to the opposing teams.

   - Each person samples (optional) one bite from each dish and votes for their favorite team's appetizer, main course, and dessert--no one can vote for their own team's creations.

How to Make a Chef Hat

- Fold 3 sheets of 10 inch by 12 inch white tissue paper in half the long way.
- Gather and tape one of the short sides of each sheet along the strip of white poster board (26 inch by 3.5 inch), overlapping the sheets slightly. Double sided tape may be used between the edges of the overlapped sheets so that they will not separate when puffed up.
- Curl the poster board band tape side out, place it around a tween's head, and paper clip the ends. Gather the tissue at the top, taping it tightly together and cutting off any excess tissue. Remove the paper clips, turn right-side out, re-attach the paper clips, and puff out the tissue.

INSTRUCTIONS ARE ALSO AVAILABLE ONLINE COURTESY OF EHOW. CO.UK - CLEAR INSTRUCTIONS ON HOW TO DO (JUST ABOUT) EVERYTHING. *HTTP://WWW.EHOW.COM/HOW_5170215_MAKE-CHILDS-CHEF-HAT.HTML#IXZZ28KH1JEPN*

6. Award Prizes

   - Tally votes.
   - Award prizes to the winning team of each course.
   - Invite contestants and their parents to sample left-over dishes.

7. Clean up. This may take some time!

Materials Used

   - White poster board
   - White tissue paper
   - Tape
   - Paper Clips
   - Microwave
   - 5 Microwavable plates
   - 5 Microwavable bowls
   - Water (for boiling)
   - Plastic bowls
   - Paper plates
   - Napkins
   - Tablecloths
   - Knives/forks/spoons
   - Skewers
   - Butter/margarine
   - Marshmallows
   - Rice cereal
   - Taco shells
   - Jam
   - Ham slices
   - Instant noodles
   - Ice cream cones

- Bananas
- Potatoes
- Bread
- Chocolate syrup
- Strawberry syrup
- Whipping cream
- Sprinkles
- Chocolate chips
- Crackers
- Canned fruit
- Caramel sauce
- Graham crackers

Budget

Approximately $120. Some supplies do not spoil, so leftovers can be used again.

General Comments

This program was such a hit that we have already offered it twice! Some of the parents came in after the program to sample their child's culinary concoction. Caution: This program is not for those with a weak stomach, as the tweens will definitely want you to sample their creations as well!

A Wee Bit O' Fun

While the older set may celebrate St. Patrick's Day by partaking in various libations, we celebrate it at the library in a safe and fun fashion! This is a creative Irish-themed party in which green is very important. Wear green, serve green food and punch, and have games that center around green, Irish, and St. Paddy's themes.

Program Advertisement

Celebrate St. Patrick's Day with crafts, Irish ping pong, and other exciting activities. Will you have the luck of the Irish? For tweens ages 10-14. Registration is limited. Free registration at any branch.

Number of Spaces Available

20-30 (this will vary depending on your materials)

Program Preparation (1 hour)

1. Hide chocolate coins throughout room.

2. Generate word searches using Discovery Education's Free Puzzlemaker at *http://www.discovery-education.com/free-puzzlemaker/* or Variety Games' *http://www.puzzle-maker.com/WS/index.htm.* Make copies.

3. Set tables with the items needed for Irish Ping Pong, St. Paddy's Cards, and Word Search.

Room Set-Up

4 tables for crafts and events

Program Outline

1. Icebreaker: Select a favorite icebreaker from Chapter 2.

2.   Craft: Make shamrock St. Paddy's cards using a green pepper as a stamp.

3.   Activities

  • Irish Ping Pong: Fill clear plastic cups with water that is dyed green. The tweens compete by tossing ping pong balls into the cups. Whoever gets the most balls in the cups wins.

  • Looking for a Pot of Gold: Tweens search for the hidden chocolate coins.

  • Word Search.

4.   Award/raffle prizes, if available.

5.   Clean up.

Materials Used

  • Chocolate coins
  • Green peppers
  • Green paint, green crayons or markers
  • Paper
  • Word searches
  • Plastic Cups
  • Green Food Colouring

Budget

We spent less than $20.00 for this event. The expense depends on how many prizes you have or if you want more activities.

General Comments

Irish Ping Pong is very similar to a popular game on the show *Minute to Win It* so you can compare it to that. It's basically tic-tac-toe with cups and ping pong balls. Arrange 9 cups in a 3 by 3 block and position tweens on opposite sides of the table. Each tween receives a different colored ball and the first one with three in a row wins.The tweens really got into the competitive aspect and enjoyed the craft.

Ukrainian Egg Decorating

Nothing beats the excitement of decorating and dyeing a basketful of colorful eggs to celebrate the Easter season. And just because tweens have grown up doesn't mean this tradition has to end. In fact, with their improved dexterity and abilities comes the opportunity to explore a new art form: psyanky, or Ukrainian Easter eggs. Psyanka (singular, pronounced *py-sahn-kah*) is an egg that is decorated with Ukrainian folk design using a wax-resist method. Traditional pysanky are very symbolic, with images and colors representing a variety of meanings. But the real fun for tweens comes in creating their own unique and meaningful designs!

Program Advertisement

Learn how to decorate eggs Ukrainian style! Each tween can bring one hard-boiled egg for practice. All other materials, including hollowed eggs, will be provided. Please wear old, short-sleeved clothing. Space is limited.

Number of Spaces Available

This depends on how many volunteers and/or staff are on hand to assist. 15-20 participants would be a recommended maximum.

Program Preparation

1. Before you choose to offer this program, check library policy to ensure that it is feasible, as psyanky often requires the use of candles and open flame. There are electric kystka/styluses available, however these are expensive and probably won't fit your budget.

2. Decide if you are doing the psyanky yourself or locating a local expert. Because this is such an intense program, it is recommended that an external facilitator be used. To find an expert, contact any Ukrainian cultural clubs, churches or student organizations (college and university level) that might be located nearby. Or, search the Internet to see if any other psyanky workshops have been held in your area. If so, contact the organization to find out who the facilitator was. You will likely find that most psyanky artists have held workshops before and have program parameters well established. Many artists have also invested in sets of electric styluses which will eliminate the need for open flame.

3. If you are running the program yourself, there are many kits available for purchase online. Be forewarned that they can be quite pricey. If you are going to invest in kits, you might want to offer this program multiple times and at multiple locations to get your money's worth. To order online, try BabasBeeswax (*www.babasbeeswax.com*) or Psyanky USA (*www.pysankyusa.com*). In addition to dyes and waxes, you will also need to purchase a kystka (stylus) for each participant.

4. For detailed, step-by-step instructions on how to create psyanky, visit LearnPsyanky.com (*www.learnpysanky.com*).

5. Pull any books the library may have on psyanky.

6. Print psyanky designs and examples. Print the meaning of symbols and colors, available online at *http://www.docstoc.com/docs/79019985/Ukranian-Folk-Art-of-Pysanky-Colors-and-Symbols-%E2%80%A2-Here-are-some*.

.

Room Set-up

1-2 tables set up as a dyeing station

Tables and chairs for participants to use as a work station. Do not overcrowd.

Program Outline

1. Ensure that all participants are wearing short-sleeved shirts/rolled-up shirt sleeves and have all long hair tied back to prevent exposure to open flames.

2. Stress the importance of proper behaviour near the candles.

3. Explain the meaning of symbols and colors.

4. Begin decorating eggs. When the eggs are complete, remove the wax and apply a gloss or varnish if desired. If the decorating takes too long, tweens may opt to leave their egg at the library for you to varnish. Arrange a day and time for tweens to pick up their creation.

5. Clean up.

Materials Used

- Large or extra-large chicken eggs (either room temperature or hollowed)
- Stylus/kystka
- Assorted colors of dye
- Water
- White vinegar
- Kettle
- Spoons
- Jars
- Beeswax
- Candles/lighters
- Pencils
- Thick elastics (for straight lines)
- Paper towel
- Gloss/varnish
- Newspapers/tablecloths
- Books about pysanky
- Design print-outs for inspiration

Budget

This depends on if you have an outside artist come to your library or if you buy all the materials yourself. We paid approximately $150, or $10 per tween, for an artist to teach the class. This included all materials.

General Comments

This is a great, unique program to offer in the Spring or even at Christmas. Because psyanky is such a rare form of art, it is an exciting experience for tweens. To keep things running smoothly, be sure to have extra volunteers, staff or students on hand. It is also helpful to have one or two people in charge of the dyeing station, dipping eggs into the dye in an orderly fashion. This will alleviate spills and disasters. Even though this program is a bit pricey and can be stressful if you are running it yourself, it is a lot of fun and will certainly have tweens coming back for more! Also, make sure you have enough time to set up, run the program, and clean up. Our artist took everyone's eggs home to complete the last phase (putting varnish on) and brought them back for tweens to pick up at the library. We've also offered this as a program for tweens and their parents at the same time. It always fills up.

80s Party

You can celebrate any decade in a party format. It's super fun – and the best part is putting together an awesome costume! We picked 80s because the tweens seemed fascinated with this decade. This party has a great deal of flexibility.

Program Advertisement

Get out those leg warmers and neon clothing because the 80s are back! You are invited to this, like, totally rad party. Dress in classic 80s garb, because we are having a costume contest that everyone will be talking about! There will be awesome 80s music, munchies, and more. Register at any branch.

Number of Spaces Available

20-30 or more, depending on your space

Program Preparation (2-3 hours)

1. For the 80s celebrity match-up, print photos of 80s stars and label each with a number. Pin to the walls throughout the room. Create and print a list of the chosen celebrity's names. Scramble the order so they don't correspond with the numbers on the wall.

2. Prepare for the MacGyver Challenge by filling bags with random objects that MacGyver might use: string, garbage bags, water bottle, stapler, tape dispenser, pen, etc.

1980s Matching Game!
Match the totally 80s star to their poster!

___	Michael Jackson	___	The A Team
___	Popples	___	David Bowie
___	Madonna	___	Degrassi
___	Michael J. Fox	___	The Goonies
___	Molly Ringwald	___	John Cusack
___	Punky Brewster	___	Corey Feldman

1980s Trivia

- **Section One - earn one point for each correct answer**

True or False?

1. The cat in *The Smufs* was named Azrial.   _____

2. The bully in *Diff'rent Strokes* was known as The Gooch.   _____

3. *The Jeffersons* was a spin off of *The Facts of Life*.   _____

4. Pierre Trudeau was Prime Minister from 1981-1987.   _____

5. Mt. St. Helens erupted in 1980.   _____

- **Section Two - earn two points for each correct answer**

Multiple Choice

1. Who did Magic Johnson play for throughout the 1980s?
   A. Orlando Magic   B. Toronto Raptors   C. LA Lakers

2. Who had an 80s Number One Hit with *Karma Chameleon*?
   A. Culture Club   B. The Go Gos   C. Bananarama

3. What was Michael Jackson advertising when he was nearly killed?
   A. Coca Cola   B. Pepsi   C. 7-Up

4. Which one of the following foods were introduced in the 1980s?
   A. Burrito   C. McNuggets   C. The Whopper

5. What was the name of the *Dukes of Hazzard's* car?

   A. Colonel Smith   B. General Lee   C. Lieutenant Dan

- **Bonus - answer this question correctly and receive 5 points**

Frankie Goes To Hollywood was a popular band in the 1980's. What is the title to one of their songs?

_____

3. Print 80s Trivia

4. Set up for the Coke vs. Pepsi Challenge:

    - Label 20-30 disposable Coke-filled cups with the letter A.

    - Label 20-30 disposable Pepsi-filled cups with the letter B.

Room Set-Up

Several tables for 80s stations

Post pictures of 80s icons period throughout the room for the celebrity match-up..

Decorate 80s style – think neon! Remember 80s classic movies like *Breakfast Club* and *Pretty in Pink* for inspiration. Decorate the room with brightly colored balloons and streamers.

Play 80s music throughout program. If you're not familiar with the decade's greatest hits, check out the Billboard Top Hits for that year at Like Totally 80s Billboard Number One Hits, *http://www. liketotally80s.com/billboard-number-one-hits.html.*

MacGyver Challenge

MacGyver, or Mac as he is known to his friends, is an intelligent, resourceful secret agent. He works for the Phoenix Foundation in Los Angeles and is educated as a scientist with a background as a bomb team technician. MacGyver does not believe in solving crime with violence and refuses to use a gun. He does, however, use his trusty Swiss Army knife and common household items, together with his vast scientific knowledge in his fight against injustice. Often his quick thinking allows him use those common objects to come up with complex devices in a matter of minutes and get out of life-or-death situations.

Challenge: Your team was exploring the library and became trapped in the scary stacks! No doors work. All you can see is books for miles and miles. How do you get out?
Ask yourself: What would MacGyver do? You have 10 minutes to make a plan. You can only use the everyday items in your bag to escape.

Program Outline

1. Icebreaker: Select a favorite icebreaker from Chapter 3.

2. 80s Matching Game
   - Tweens pick up a quiz when they get their name tags.
   - Tweens match the picture to the celebrity, movie, or musician.

3. Rubik's Cube Contest
   - Give each player a Rubik's cube or put tweens in teams and pass out one full size Rubik's cube per team.
   - Players attempt to solve the puzzle by the end of the program.

4. Dancing Contest
   - Cut 2 cardboard boxes flat and lay out on the floor.
   - Teach moves first: snaking, moon walking, the running man, Cabbage Patch, the surf. Not familiar with break dancing moves? You can show the moves on YouTube, search "How to Breakdance." All tweens who want to participate in the contest will have 60 seconds to perform their best breakdancing moves.
   - Tweens vote for the best dancer and the winner will receive a prize.

5. MacGyver Challenge
   - Briefly discuss the premise of the show *MacGyver*.
   - Separate tweens into teams.
   - Hand out the random objects bags and read the "MacGyver" scenario to the group.
   - Each group will have 5 minutes to come up with an escape plan, using only the items in their bag.
   - The team with the most elaborate escape plan wins! You can decide the winner or have the tweens vote.

6. Activity Stations
   - 80s trivia handout
   - Board games (Trouble, Operation)
   - Pepsi challenge
     - Tweens taste each cola and decide which is Pepsi, writing their names and answers on a scrap piece of paper.
     - Reveal the answer at the end of the program, awarding a small prize to those who answer correctly.
   - Make your Own Leg Warmers
   - 80s Version of the Nintendo Game system (NES)

7.   Clean up.

Materials Used

- 80s Trivia
- Disposable cups
- MacGyver Challenge items
- Leg-warmer instructions
- Streamers
- Pencils
- Coke and Pepsi
- Scrap paper for Pepsi Challenge
- Scissors sharp enough to cut fabric
- Sweaters/sweatpants for leg-warmers (donations/thrift store)
- Board games
- NES system and games

Budget

This depends on how many activities you do, what kind of materials you have around the library to use or if you or the staff have any 80s items.

General Comments

There are a lot of ideas on the Internet on how to throw a 1980s themed party that you can modify for your own event. Begin your search here *http://www.partymall.com/party_ideas/creative_party/1980s_party* or here

http://www.ehow.com/list_6957490_suggestions-throw-1980s-party.html.

How to Make Leg Warmers

Winter is almost here, and for the fashion forward, that means you have to start getting really creative to keep warm while staying stylish. Wearing legwarmers over your jeans or <u>tights</u> (if you're wearing a skirt) is a good way to keep extra warm.
On top of that, legwarmers are back in the spotlight, featured in many designers' collections for this winter and on sale at lots of popular stores. Did you know, though, that there are several different ways to make your own? All are really easy!

Sweatpants make perfect no-<u>sew</u> legwarmers. All you have to do is buy a pair in a color you like, and cut off the legs somewhere above the knee. It's that simple, because sweatpants do not need to be hemmed. Just flip them over and put them on, cuff first. Your look is complete, and it only took five minutes!

Another option is to make legwarmers out of the arms of a <u>sweatshirt</u>. This works nearly exactly the same way, but makes much smaller, less baggy legwarmers.

There are other items of clothing that lend themselves beautifully to the creation of legwarmers: make them from the arms of a sweater you don't want anymore, or one you got at a thrift store.

Cutting a sweater can be tricky, and you'll probably need to hem the cut edge, to prevent the whole thing from unravelling. Thermal pants also make great legwarmers, and like the sweatpants, don't need to be hemmed. You can get thermals inexpensively at just about any large store like Wal-mart or Costco, or at most sporting goods stores.

Chapter 7: April

The smell of spring is in the air and with the rejuvenation that it brings, comes great library programming! When program planning for toddlers and pre-schoolers, there are tons of Spring and April related themes to choose from, however, trying to come up with something cool enough for tweens takes a bit more creativity. Here are four sure-fire programs that fit the bill: Mythbusters, Party Like an April Fool, Poetry Pwnage, and an 8th Grade Grad Expo!

Mythbusters

Based on the Discovery Channel's popular television show, *Mythbusters,* this program challenges tweens to use their scientific skills to determine whether or not a variety of proposed statements are true, or if they are, in fact, myths. Tweens then have the opportunity to test their hypothesis with fun activities and experiments. This program is a great way to showcase your collection of science experiment books, and to make tweens aware of the excellent resources available for the always dreaded science fair project assignment. If you are unfamiliar with the *Mythbusters* television show, more information is available online at *http://dsc.discovery.com/fansites/mythbusters/about/about.html.*

Program Advertisement

Do you have what it takes to be a mythbuster? Think it's as easy as it looks on TV? Come to the library and debunk a myth, like "Can an egg bounce?"

COURTESY OF OSHAWA PUBLIC LIBRARIES GRAPHICS DEPARTMENT

Number of Spaces Available

30 spaces

Program Preparation (1 hour)

1.   Soak 3 dozen eggs in vinegar for at least 24 hours.

2.   Prepare a "slime" mixture for each team: Mix one cup of corn starch and ½ cup of water. Add a few drops of food coloring and stir with a spoon. It is easier to make five separate bowls of slime rather than one big recipe.

3. Cut up slips of paper for tweens to record their hypothesis, three for each tween.

4. Gather books about structures, both general and specific buildings (Eiffel Tower, bridges, etc.).

5. Find a science DVD, such as *Bill Nye the Science Guy* (Disney Educational).

Room Set-up

5 tables with 6 chairs around each

Program Outline

1. Icebreaker: Since this program is all about facts and myths, ask tweens to play "Two Truths and a Lie," as outlined in chapter 3.

2. Form Teams: Divide tweens into teams of three.

3. Explain the Rules

   - Follow directions.

   - Work together as a team and take turns.

   - Keep your hands to yourself (as they will get very messy!).

   - Three myths will be presented and it is your job to figure out if they are "confirmed" or "busted."

4. Myth 1: Paper Can Support a Book. Ask each team to write either "confirmed" or "busted" on a slip of paper. Once this is done, it's time to experiment! Hand each team a book about structures for some inspiration, a sheet of paper, a lightweight book, and a piece of clear tape. Allow each team approximately five minutes to prove their theory. Award one point to each team that has the correct answer. In this case, the myth is confirmed! Fold a piece of paper accordion style and a book will rest on it, or roll the paper into a tube using a piece of tape, and a book will also rest on it.

5. Myth 2: Eggs Cannot Bounce. Ask each team to write either "confirmed" or "busted" on a slip of paper. Once this is done, it's time to experiment! Hand each team-member an egg that has been soaked in vinegar for at least 24 hours. Do not tell the tweens about this process. Allow each team-member the chance to bounce the egg, starting low to the table and working their way higher. See how high each tween can go before the egg breaks. Award one point to each team that has the correct answer. In this case, the myth is busted! Explain that the calcium from the egg and the acid from the vinegar create a chemical reaction, causing carbon dioxide to be released. Once all of the carbon is released from the egg, it will bounce. A video of this experiment is available online at *http://www.youtube.com/watch?v=GrVuag3YCtQ&feature=related*.

6. Myth 3: A Substance Can Be a Solid and Liquid at the Same Time. Ask each team to write either "confirmed" or "busted" on a slip of paper. Once this is done, it's time to experiment! Hand each team a bowl of prepared slime. Ask team members to alternately take turns punching and running their hands through the mixture. Award one point to each team that has the correct answer. In this

case, the myth is confirmed! Explain that the cornstarch and water mix is an example of suspension. When you squeeze the slime, it feels like a solid because the molecules line up. But when no one touches it, it acts as a liquid because the molecules relax. A video of this experiment is available online at *http://www.youtube.com/watch?v=fazPiaHvFcg&feature=related.*

7. Snacks and a Movie: While tweens are enjoying a snack, show a science DVD. Take this opportunity to tally points and to determine a winner.

8. Award Prizes.

9. Clean up.

Materials Used

- 3 dozen eggs
- Vinegar
- Styrofoam or plastic cups
- Cornstarch
- Green food coloring
- Water
- Spoons
- Plastic bowls
- Tablecloths
- 10 sheets of paper
- Clear tape
- 10 lightweight books
- Books about structures
- 10 pencils
- Slips of blank paper for tweens to record their hypothesis
- *Bill Nye the Science Guy* (Disney Educational) DVD
- Snacks and beverages
- Prizes

Budget

Approximately $20 for supplies and snacks

General Comments

It may seem like there aren't enough activities to fill an hour, but tweens will enjoy taking an extra-long time to play with the eggs and slime. Because it is sometimes difficult to get the consistency of the slime correct, give yourself enough time to get it right. Soak extra eggs, just in case some of the shells don't properly dissolve. Use lots of tablecloths and newspapers on the floor and make sure a sink is nearby!

Party Like an April Fool

If you haven't been able to tell, we're big on parties at our library because they are fun and can be done year-after-year in many different ways. In fact, our parties are so popular that we've been asked to host birthday parties for tweens outside of the library! For this event, wackiness and pranking are key elements. Make sure that all participants follow the Prankster's Code: No prank can be mean-spirited, dangerous, crude, or lewd.

Program Advertisement

Release your inner prankster and prepare to have fun at this party. Will you be fooled?

Number of Spaces Available

30 spaces

Program Preparation (2 hours)

1. Obtain materials for the whoopee cushion craft. A whoopee cushion is one of the oldest prank props in the book. Essentially a rubber cushion filled with air that makes a farting sound when someone sits on it, the whoopee cushion has delighted school children and adults alike since they were invented in the 1930s.

2. Prepare a Kitty Litter Cake.

3. Create Prankster Points and make copies of the Prankster Code.

4. Pull books from the collection that contain pranks or April Fools content.

5. Put a sign on the door that says "This Program is Cancelled." Then, slightly underneath, have another sign that says "NOT!" or "JUST KIDDING!"

Whoopee Cushion
Supplies:
- Rubber sheets or large balloons (from craft store)
- Rubber glue
- Scissors

How to:
Cut two matching balloon shaped pieces. The shape is basically a circle with a triangle at the bottom. Glue the rubber together leaving an opening at the bottom for air to escape. Blow into the opening to inflate the cushion. Place the cushion on an unsuspecting person's chair. Whoopee Cushion Craft instructions are also available online at *http://www.ehow.com/how_2310833_make-whoopee-cushion.html#ixzz27P8Cm4Gj*

Kitty Litter Cake
Ingredients:
- 1 unfrosted chocolate cake
- 1 unfrosted white cake
- 1 package of white sandwich cookies
- 5 white pudding cups
- 6 small Tootsie Rolls
- Green food coloring
- 1 new kitty litter pan
- 1 kitty litter scoop

Directions:
Crumble white sandwich cookies in small batches in a blender, scraping with a spatula frequently as they get sticky, or use your hands. Add a few drops of green food coloring to half the crumbled cookie bits and set aside. Crumble the cakes into a large bowl. Toss gently with half the cookie crumbs and the chilled pudding. Pour into a new, clean kitty litter box. Put unwrapped Tootsie Rolls in a microwave-safe dish two at a time and heat until soft and pliable. Shape ends so they are no longer blunt, curving slightly. Repeat with more Tootsie Rolls and bury them in the mixture. Sprinkle the other half of the cookie crumbs over top. Heat three more Tootsie Rolls in the microwave until almost melted. Scrape them on top of the cake, or even over the side of the litter box, and sprinkle with cookie crumbs. Serve with a new pooper scooper.

Room Set-up

5 tables with 6 chairs around each

Program Outline

1. Icebreaker: Since the goal of this program is to prank people, play "True or False" which is just a shortened version of "Two Truths and a Lie." See Chapter 3 for instructions.

2. Formation of Teams: Divide tweens into teams of 3-5.

Book List for Party Like an April Fool
- Buckman, Erik L. *The Prankster's Ultimate Handbook: the World's Most Infamous, Illustrated, Hardcore Guide to Fiendishly Clever Practical Jokery & Much, Much More!!* New Cents, 2004.
- Hargrave, John. *Mischief Maker's Manual.* Grosset & Dunlap, 2011.
- Rose, Alexa. *The Prankster's Handbook Pack-tivities.* Downtown Bookworks, 2011.

Can you answer these questions about some April Fools hoaxes?
1. In 1957, the BBC reported that Italians were finally able to harvest spaghetti from trees because of the removal of which pest?
   A) Flying Cats   B) *The Spaghetti Weevil*   C) Spaghetti Tree Burrowers
2. Which fast food restaurant claimed in 1996 to have purchased the U.S. Liberty Bell?
   A) McDonalds   B) *Taco Bell*   C) Burger King
3. In 2004, a television station reported that local British tap water would be:
   A) *Made diet*   B) Changed to juice   C) Shut off due to contamination
4. In 2009, *The Guardian* announced it would be the first newspaper to:
   A) Give away free computers   B) Publish weekly UFO sightings   C) *Publish exclusively on Twitter*
5. In 1997, the hosts of which two game shows switched for the day?
   A) Wheel of Fortune and Let's Make a Deal   B) *Jeopardy and Wheel of Fortune*   C) The Price is Right and Family Feud
6. In 2009, Wikipedia's homepage featured which museum?
   A) Museum of Old Things   B) Museum of Ugly Socks   C) *Museum of Bad Art*
7. In 1953, Dutch television reported that which famous landmark had fallen to the ground?
   A) *The Tower of Pisa*   B) The Eiffel Tower   C) The Colosseum
8. Which of the following in NOT a BMW hoax?
   A) MINIs sent to Mars   B) Scrolling text message machines on the front of cars   C) *All cars being equipped with boating capabilities*
9. In 2008, the BBC reported on the finding of a colony of flying:
   A) *Penguins*   B) Chickens   C) Kangaroos

3. Explain the Rules:

   - Present Prankster Code.

   - Have teams create a Prankster name.

   - Explain Prankster Points – every time a team pulls a prank or comes up with a great idea for a prank they will receive Prankster Points. At the end of the program, Prankster Points are tallied and the winning team receives prizes.

4. April Fools Trivia: Now it's time to test each team's knowledge of April Fools hoaxes. Teams must answer multiple choice questions to determine what happened in the April Fools hoax described.

5. As a joke, Microsoft® claimed to be releasing a new Xbox 360 video game about: A) *Yodeling* B) Disco Dancing   C) Pencil Sharpening

6. Create a Whoopee Cushion Craft: Everyone knows that one of the oldest pranks in the book is the Whoopee Cushion!

7. Play Twister®: What's more foolish than a game that ties you up in knots?

8. Serve snacks and play charades: While tweens are enjoying the Kitty Litter Cake (if they dare), have funny and foolish charades printed out and ready for them to perform. Alternatively, you could show a movie or TV show at this time.

9. Award Prizes: By now, many pranks must have occurred, or ideas of future pranks have been made. Count up the Prankster Points and award some foolish prizes!

10. Clean up.

Materials Used

- Rubber
- Scissors
- Glue
- Green food coloring
- Kitty Litter Box (available at dollar stores)
- Pooper Scooper
- 1 package of German chocolate cake mix (alternatively you can buy cake pre-made)
- 1 package of white cake mix
- 6 vanilla pudding cups
- 1 package of vanilla sandwich cookies
- 1 package of Tootsie Rolls®
- Paper plates
- Napkins
- Forks
- Tablecloths

- Books about pranks/hoaxes
- Twister® or another game
- Beverages
- Prizes

Budget

Approximately $25 for supplies and snacks

General Comments

Depending on the tweens' interest level, this party can go by really quickly. That's why it's good to encourage the teams to come up with lots of prankster ideas throughout the entire program, and if there is time left over at the end, come up with big pranks as a group, or tell the group famous pranks throughout history.

FOOLING AROUND AT THE PARTY LIKE AN APRIL FOOL PROGRAM. COURTESY OF OSHAWA PUBLIC LIBRARIES GRAPHICS DEPARTMENT

Poetry Pwnage

What's in a name? For this program, everything! April is poetry month, and libraries love to highlight this celebration. A program called "Poetry at the Library" or even "Magnetic Poetry" may sound dull to a tween. Kick it up a notch using slang – Poetry Pwnage! To pwn someone is to "own" or defeat them, a term typically used in the video game world. Parents and other librarians often wonder if this is a typo, but tweens know it's the real deal! A video teaching you how to pronounce pwn is available online at *http://www.youtube.com/watch?v=7rvhsxYGvV4.*

Program Advertisement

Pwn poetry in this fun competition! Compete against others as you make magnetic poetry, create a haiku, and more!

Number of Spaces Available

15 spaces

Program Preparation (1 hour)

1. Obtain materials for magnetic poetry craft. Pre-print words for the tweens to cut out and use – make lots of nouns, verbs, adjectives, conjunctions, etc. Also, have blank paper for tweens to write their own words.

2. Pull any books from the collection that are about poetry or are written in verse.

3. Pull music CDs from the collection to listen to while tweens are working on their craft; allow the tweens to vote on what they want to listen to.

Room Set-up

3 tables with 5 chairs around each

Program Outline

1. Icebreaker: Have the tweens create an acrostic poem using their name.

2. Magnetic Poetry Craft: Tweens can cut out the words you have printed and individually attach them to a magnetic strip with adhesive on one side (available at any craft store). Voila – magnetic poetry that can be moved around to create a different poem each time! Once completed, the magnetic pieces can be stuck to baking sheets, fridges, or any other object that magnets are attracted to. If there is enough time, give each tween a small tin, either new or a used Altoids container. Provide paint, sequins, stickers and foam shapes so tweens can decorate a storage box for their magnetic poetry. Detailed instructions are available online at *http://familycrafts.about.com/od/alteredar-*

tandcollage/ss/Poetry_Magnet_Craft. htm or *http://www.readwritethink. org/files/resources/activity_30150_ how-to.pdf.* Or make magnetic poetry with Avery Labels at *http://curbly. com/DIY-Maven/posts/649-Avery-Labels-Magnetic-strike-Poetry-strike-Words#jump.*

3. Haiku Battle: Explain what a haiku is and give a few examples. See who can come up with a haiku about a literary character (or whatever you prefer) the fastest. Award a prize for as many as you please: fastest, most creative, funniest, prettiest, craziest, etc.

4. Magnetic Poetry Slam

   - Either with the poetry they just created, or with actual store-bought magnetic poetry – host a slam!

   - Divide the poetry words among the tables and have tweens create poems individually or in a group.

   - If you have a microphone, pass it around the room so they can read their poems.

Haiku is a form of Japanese poetry that is written about one single subject, usually nature or seasons. Haiku poems consist of three lines that rarely rhyme. The first and third line have five syllables and the middle line has seven syllables.

Syllable: a word can be divided into syllables. Each syllable is a sound that can be said without interruption and usually consist of a vowel which can have consonants before and/or after it. Ex am ple has three syllables.

In the fresh spring breeze
How snowy is the heron
Flying through pine-trees.
- *Raizan*

In the lonely night
There the firefly glides one foot
Putting out its light
- *Hokushi*

Additional examples of haikus are available online at *http://www.kidzone.ws/poetry/haiku.htm.*

- After everyone has read their poems, have tweens switch tables or swap words to make up more poetry.

- Repeat as often as the tweens are enjoying the activity.

5. Snacks and booktalks: Serve snacks and booktalk a few books that are written in verse or have a poetry element to them. You could also show a movie or just chat.

6. Award Prizes: If you haven't already awarded prizes for the earlier pwnages, do so now.

7. Clean up.

Materials Used

- Paper
- Markers
- Pens

- Magnetic tape
- Scissors
- Paint
- Paintbrushes
- Sequins
- Foam shapes
- Stickers
- Haiku examples
- Poetry books
- Snacks
- Beverages
- Prizes

Budget

Approximately $20 for supplies and snacks

General Comments

This program can be part of a larger poetry workshop if you have many tweens who are interested in creative writing. Or, if tweens in your area are more inclined to attend craft programs, market it as such to draw a larger audience.

8th Grade Grad Expo

Agree with it or not, 8th grade graduation celebrations have grown to epic proportions, often rivaling high school proms and even some weddings. Boys are buying or renting suits and tuxedos; girls are buying fancy dresses, and getting their hair and make-up done. Some tweens are even renting limos! While tweens get caught up in the glitz and glamor, parents often don't know where to begin. An expo at the library can be the perfect starting point. And the great part is, just like graduation celebrations, you can make this program as basic or as glamorous as you wish! From simple, in-house workshop stations, to a showcase of local vendors, the sky is the limit! Since we exhibited a variety of vendors, this program outline will focus on that particular format.

Program Advertisement

Don't know what to wear to 8th Grade Grad? We can help! Find all of your grad needs at the 8th Grade Grad Expo on _____ (insert date and time). Join us for an afternoon/evening of glitz, glam, fashion and more with ideas for both guys and girls! Everyone who attends will get a chance to win fabulous prizes!

Number of Spaces Available

Exhibitors: as many as your space will allow but we suggest a maximum of 15

Tweens and parents: unlimited

Program Preparation (4-5 hours)

1. Determine a date, time, and location for the program. We suggest an evening or weekend. Since most companies do not want to set-up a booth for only an hour or two, we recommend a four hour program. Tweens and their parents are welcome to drop-by at any point within this timeframe. In terms of location, you may choose to put all vendors in one room, or to scatter them throughout the library.

2. Decide what your library can offer each vendor as an incentive for participating. This will likely be advertising. Not only are tweens and their parents getting information about their store and service at the event, but their logo can be included in all print materials used to advertise the event. Don't forget the power of your library website, Facebook page, and Twitter account to advertise your event and their involvement in it. If you are able to do mail outs to area schools, include company logos.

3. Figure out the room set-up so you know exactly how many vendors you can invite. Decide the maximum number of tables each vendor can request. Most vendors will only want one, however they may require a larger space for clothing racks, make-up chairs and other props. Make sure you reserve a table for the library to display books and to collect passports.

4. Decide if you want to include a fashion show as part of this event. If so, a "runway" and seating will have to be included in the room set-up.

5. Research local companies that provide goods and services that tweens might use to prepare for their graduation. Check the telephone book, search online, or get word of mouth recommendations. Create a document or spreadsheet with contact information for each shop or service provider. This will be especially useful if you offer this program a second or third time.

Possible Vendors:
Hairstylist
Make-up artist
Nail salon
Florist
Dress shop
Seamstress (for tweens wanting a custom made dress)
Shoe store
Suit and/or tuxedo rentals
Limousine company
Photographer
Gift shop
Jewellery or accessory store

6. Approximately six months before the event, contact each potential vendor by phone to gauge their level of interest. Typically, independent shops and small business are more willing to attend, as they have more to gain by advertising their company. If companies are interested in becoming a vendor, send them an information booklet and contract. You may also choose to charge vendors a small amount to help cover the cost of advertising or snacks. We charged each vendor $30. Or, you may wish to charge a refundable deposit to ensure that vendors show-up on the day of the expo.

8ᵗʰ Grade Grad Expo

Date

Time

VENDOR EXHIBITION

8ᵗʰ Grade Grad Expo

Public Libraries invites you to exhibit at the 1st Annual 8th Grade Grad Expo to be held _____
(date and time).

WHO SHOULD EXHIBIT

The 8ᵗʰ Grade Grad Expo is an opportunity for the community to meet and greet local vendors of graduation related products and services, as well as a chance for vendors to advertise and generate business. The purpose of this event is to meet the informational needs of the community and provide an educational opportunity for tweens and their parents. Companies that offer any goods or services that help in graduation preparations, such as (but not limited to): fashion, florists, photographers, jewelry, gifts, limo services and much more.

EXHIBIT INFORMATION

We request one donation per vendor to be awarded as door prizes. Please bring your door prize on the day of the event.

The Vendor Fee is <u>$30</u>.
- Each vendor is required to pay a $30 non-refundable fee and attach it to a completed registration form in order to reserve a table at the expo.

- Space will be assigned according to the order in which payment is received.

- There are a limited number of electrical outlets. Any special requests for access to these outlets will be accommodated and assigned according to the order in which payment is received.

- The library will accept money orders, cash and personal cheques made payable to _____.

The library will provide one 6' x 30" table, two chairs and linens. We will also have refreshments for the vendors prior to and during the event. Due to space limitations freight cannot be shipped for storage prior to the 8ᵗʰ Grade Grad Expo. There will be several short information session time slots available. The format of these sessions can be varied. For example: selecting an audience member to have their hair and make-up done on stage or discussing color trends in dresses, etc. If you are interested in a conducting a session, please indicate on the registration form and more details will follow.

EXHIBIT SCHEDULE

2:45pm – 3:45pm LIBRARY SPACE OPEN FOR SET UP

4:00pm – 8:00pm EXHIBIT OPEN TO THE PUBLIC (information session schedule TBA)

8:00pm – 9:00pm TAKE DOWN AND CLEAN UP

Please arrive in enough time to set up your area. No early take-downs or clean-ups

8th Grade Grad Expo

EXHIBITOR REGISTRATION

COMPANY NAME: _____

CONTACT PERSON: _____

COMPANY ADDRESS: _____

PHONE: _____

CELL:_____

EMAIL: _____

DESCRIPTION OF GOODS/SERVICES:

_____

_____

DOOR PRIZE DESCRIPTION:

_____

_____

____ I HAVE ATTACHED THE VENDOR FEE
____ I AM INTERESTED IN CONDUCTING AN INFORMATION SESSION
____ I NEED AN ELECTRICAL OUTLET
____ I / WE HAVE READ AND AGREE TO ABIDE BY THE RULES AND
      REGULATIONS OF THE EVENT (ATTACHED):

AUTHORIZED SIGNATURE _____

TITLE_____ DATE_____

Please send registration form and payment attention to:
Name, Position,
Library, Address, Phone Number, Email Address
A confirmation email will be sent to you upon receipt of your registration.

7. Ask each vendor to donate a door prize, one of which will be used as a grand prize.

8. As paperwork and contracts are returned, assign each vendor a table. If you have multiple vendors for the same service, try to put them at opposite ends of the room. Send each vendor a receipt if you are charging a deposit or fee.

9. Create all publicity items and post wherever you can. Send mail outs to schools and other community agencies that serve tweens. Send copies of all advertisement to the vendors to be posted in their stores and on their websites. Include any specific times for fashion shows or other scheduled components.

10. Create a passport that lists all vendors.

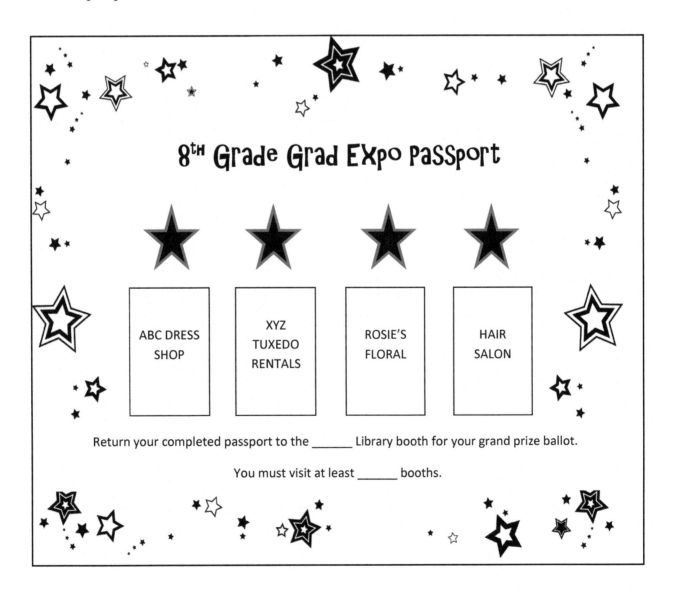

11. A week prior to the expo, contact vendors to remind them of the event and to firm up any last minute details.

12. Order or purchase a snack tray for vendors (veggies, fruit, cheese and crackers)

13. Set-up tables, putting the appropriate vendor's name on each.

14. Assign someone to greet each vendor, ensuring this person knows where each vendors table is located.

15. Assign someone to record the number of tweens and parents attending the expo and to greet expo guests.

16. Set-up a vendor lounge area, where vendors can eat a snack.

17. Set-up the library booth, displaying books about fashion, hair, make-up, and corsages and boutonnieres.

Information to Include for Vendors
Address and map of location
Arrival time
Unloading instructions
Parking instructions
Size of table and/or display space
What the library will provide (tablecloths, electrical outlets, table, chairs, etc.)
What the vendor must supply (items for display, display props, etc.)
Availability of food and beverages

Room Set-up

Tables and chairs for vendors

A table and chairs in a designated "vendor lounge"

Program Outline

1. When vendors arrive, make sure they have everything they need. Collect any door prizes they are donating.

2. As tweens and parents arrive, have them fill out a ballot for a door prize. Depending on the number of door prizes you receive, you may wish to do a draw every thirty minutes. Be sure to mention each donors name several times when announcing winners to further promote each vendors business.

3. Give each tween a passport that lists all vendors. This way no vendors will be missed.

4. Draw for the grand prize.

5. Thank vendors for coming and assist them with any cleanup.

6. Contact door prize and grand prize winners via phone or email if they were not present during the draws.

7. Clean up.

8. Refund any deposits that you may have collected before the event.

Materials Used

- Refreshments for vendors
- Receipt book
- Door counter (optional)
- Ballots
- Ballot box
- Table linens (optional)
- Stamps or pens for each vendor (if a passport is being used)

Budget

Approximately $50

General Comments

If you worry that you won't have enough tweens interested in attending this event, consider expanding it to appeal to a wider audience. Since most of these vendors cater to prom-goers too, open it up to teens getting ready to attend these junior and senior rites of passage. Or, if you want to go really big, host an event expo, which would include weddings and anyone working in the event industry. You might also choose to offer an 8th Grade Grad expo on a smaller scale. This could simply consist of a makeup or nail workshop. See if a make-up artist is willing to volunteer their time to teach tweens these skills.

Chapter 8 May

Hooray…it's the merry month of May! What better way to make merry than with library programs designed to celebrate and honor the traditions of the month. We offer you Free Comic Book Day festivities, celebrated on the first Saturday of the month; a program honoring Maia, the ancient Greek goddess of spring; a floatastic fun food program; and the decoration of a trendy home for baby birds.

Greek Out!

Ideas for this program were first compiled and created during the height of Rick Riordan's popular series of novels featuring the hero Percy Jackson. With the more universal theme of ancient Greece, this program is extremely versatile and is appropriate to offer year-round, year after year. It is also a terrific way to celebrate the Summer Olympics, which can be traced back to Greece in 776 BC. The study of Greek gods and goddesses are a popular component of the school curriculum, so this educational, yet fun program will be sure to draw a lot of tweens to the library!

Program Advertisement

Join us at this Camp Half-Blood Regional Meeting as we celebrate the upcoming *Percy Jackson and the Olympians* movie! Have fun learning Ancient Greek, forging a warrior's shield, fashioning Greek sandals, togas, and more!

Number of Spaces Available

20

Program Preparation (1 hour)

1. Print the Greek alphabet chart.

Symbol	Letter	Symbol	Letter
A α	Alpha	N ν	Nu
B β	Beta	Ξ ξ	Xi
Γ γ	Gamma	O o	Omicron
Δ δ	Delta	Π π	Pi
E ε	Epsilon	P ρ	Rho
Z ζ	Zeta	Σ σ ς	Sigma
H η	Eta	T τ	Tau
Θ θ	Theta	Y υ	Upsilon
I ι	Iota	Φ φ	Phi
K κ	Kappa	X χ	Chi
Λ λ	Lambda	Ψ ψ	Psi
M μ	Mu	Ω ω	Omega

2. Using Bristol board and a paper fastener, construct a wheel that features the names of Greek gods and goddesses with an arrow for a spinner. The Titans ruled the earth before the Olympians overthrew them. The ruler of the Titans was Cronus who was dethroned by his son Zeus, an Olympian.

3. Pull books on Greek gods and goddesses, or ensure that library catalogues are reserved for program use.

4. Collect an assortment of cardboard pieces for shields.

5. Print a Medusa head for each tween.

6. Print pictures of Ancient Greek sandals, or pull books from your own collection that feature pictures of Ancient Greek footwear.

7. Print pictures of various togas, or pull books from your own collection that feature pictures of Greek togas.

The Titans

- Prometheus - Stole fire from Zeus and the gods.
- Atlas - Punished by Zeus and made to carry the sky upon his shoulders.
- Gaea - The Earth goddess.
- Uranus - The Sky god.
- Cronus - Ruler of the Titans and the father of Zeus. Associated with the harvest.
- Oceanus - Represented the Atlantic Ocean. Half man, half serpent.
- Mnemosyne - Goddess of memory and the mother of the Muses (poetry, history, dance, music, comedy, tragedy, hymns, astronomy).
- Themis - The god of justice and order.
- Coeus - The Titan of wisdom.
- Phoebe - Associated with the moon.
- Crius - Titan of the stars and constellations.
- Hyperion - Means "he who goes before the sun."
- Metis - The goddess of wisdom and deep thought.

The Olympians

- Aphrodite - Goddess of love and beauty.
- Apollo - The god of light, poetry, and music.
- Ares - God of war.
- Artemis - Goddess of the moon, forest, all animals, and the hunt.
- Athena - Goddess of wisdom, war, and arts and crafts.
- Hades - God of the Underworld.
- Hephaestus - God of fire.
- Hera - Wife of Zeus. Goddess of marriage and family.
- Hermes - The messenger of the gods, god of thieves and games.
- Hestia - Goddess of the home and family.
- Poseidon - God of the sea and earthquakes.
- Zeus - King of the gods, god of the sky, symbolized by the thunderbolt. Zeus watched over the other gods to ensure they weren't exceeding their powers.

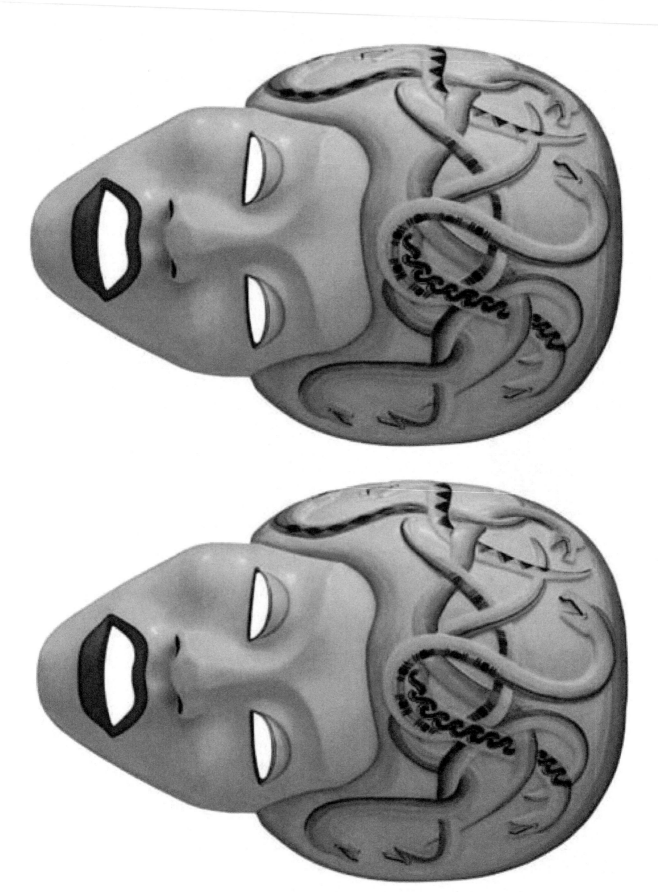

Print one Medusa head for each tween. Cut out images can be glued to each tween's shield.

8. Print or die-cut leaves, approximately ten leaves per tween for laurel wreaths.

Room Set-up

Tables and chairs for activities

An open space for the Toga Party

Program Outline

1. Icebreaker: Ask tweens to state their names and what super powers they would like to have, since all Greek gods and goddesses have a super power.

2. Learn Ancient Greek: Distribute copies of the Ancient Greek alphabet so that tweens can write their names on nametags. If the letter that they need is not part of the Greek alphabet, tweens can make up their own letter.

3. Consult the Oracle: Each tween should spin the wheel to see which Greek god or goddess claims them.

4. Find Your Story: Now that each tween has a god or goddess to claim them, it is time to do some research. Teach tweens how to use the library catalogue to find books about their god or goddess, or to save time, pull books and have them available for the tweens to peruse. Ask tweens to make point-form notes about their research so that they can share any interesting facts with the group. Tweens who have the same god or goddess may wish to work together, especially if there are not enough books to go around.

5. Forging a Warrior's Shield: Since every god and goddess needs protection, they need to have shields. Each tween should cut a shield out of cardboard and affix a Medusa head to it (in the Percy Jackson novels, Thalia has a magic shield with Medusa molded onto the front). Shields can be decorated as each tween desires and Duct Tape handles can be added.

6. Sandal-Making: Using pictures for inspiration each tween should make a pair of sandals using cardboard, fabric, Duct Tape, leather cording, or Gimp®.

7. Toga Party! No god or goddess would be complete without a toga, Randomly select half of the tweens to be "dressed" and the other half to be "dressers." Using a roll of toilet paper and pictures for inspiration, each pair fashions a toga.

8. Crown the Winner: In Ancient Greece, winners and athletic champions were often awarded a laurel wreath. Using pipe cleaners and paper leaves, each tween makes a wreath to wear.

9. Clean up.

Materials Used

- Markers
- Blank nametags
- Blank sheets of paper
- Pencils
- Spinning wheel or Bristol board and paper fasteners
- Cardboard
- Scissors
- Glue
- Duct Tape
- Cardboard
- Fabric
- Leather cording or Gimp®
- Toilet paper
- Pipe cleaners
- Cardstock for laurel leaves

Budget

$0-$20. Most of the materials used were from existing library supplies. Duct tape and toilet paper are the major expenses.

General Comments

This program was such a success that it was offered multiple times at multiple library branches! It was especially surprising to see how interested the tweens were in researching their Greek god or goddess. In fact, this took so much time that only a few of the planned activities were able to be completed, resulting in the need for additional programs!

Additional information about the Percy Jackson series and other Percy Jackson library program ideas are available online:

Disney Hyperion. "Percy Ultimate Party Kit." *Percy Jackson and the Olympians.* http://www.percyjacksonbooks.com/pdfs/Percy%20Ultimate%20Party%20Kit.pdf

Wilbur, Maren. "Compilation for Percy Jackson Program." *PUBYAC.* https://mail.lis.illinois.edu/hypermail/public/pubyac/20500.html.

Penguin Books Ltd. "PJ Teachers Pack." *Percy Jackson Books by Rick Riordan.* http://www.percyjackson.co.uk/download/pj_teachers_pack.pdf.

Manga Mania

In honor of Free Comic Book Day (the first saturday in May each year), we decided to have some manga fun! Tweens received free comic books, learned about different kinds of manga, competed in trivia for prizes and watched *Naruto!* You could show any kind of anime you'd like, or another superhero or comic book-themed movie, just check that you're licensed to show it. Contact your local independently-owned comic book store to see if you can receive free comics to give away. For more information about Free Comic Book Day, visit *http://www.freecomicbookday.com.*

Program Advertisement

Celebrate Free Comic Book Day with the (insert library name here)! Discuss your favorite manga, make Candy Sushi, and watch anime based on the coolest manga around!

Number of Spaces Available

20

Program Preparation (3 hours)

1. Create a manga presentation for those that may be unfamiliar with it. A sample presentation is available online at *https://sites.google.com/site/thetweenscene/.*

2. Create a Jeopardy-style Powerpoint that is devoted to manga. There are many templates online. You can find a template online at *http://www.rhonnold.com/JeopardyGames.html.*

3. Pull manga books to display.

4. Buy supplies for candy sushi.

5. Contact comic shops for donations of manga or comic books.

6. Decide if you'd like to watch a movie and research licensing.

Room Set-up

Tables and chairs for activities and making Candy Sushi

Projector and screen for presentations

Program Outline

1. Icebreaker: The tweens play two truths and a lie, see Chapter 3.

2. Learn about Manga: Show a presentation about manga and the different genres of manga. This is especially helpful if you're doing a trivia game and some of the tweens aren't as familiar with manga as others are. See *https://sites.google.com/site/thetweenscene/* for the presentation.

3. Discussion: Lead a discussion about manga and ask the tweens: What do you like about manga? Who is your favorite character/series? Who can name the most manga genres?

COURTESY OF OSHAWA PUBLIC LIBRARIES GRAPHICS DEPARTMENT.

4. Trivia: This is where a Powerpoint would be very useful and as listed above, there are many templates found online, such as: *http://www.rhonnold.com/JeopardyGames.html.* You can make some topics harder than others for the more seasoned manga fans.

5. Candy Sushi: Not everyone likes sushi, but almost everyone likes candy sushi! An incredibly popular activity, we find that candy sushi making is versatile and useful in many programs! Using puffed rice cereal treats, fruit wraps, and an assortment of gummy and/or licorice candies, teach tweens to make their own sushi rolls. You may make your own rice cereal treats or purchase pre-packaged varieties. Provide plastic bags so that tweens can take the extra sushi pieces home. Serve beverages as tweens sample their creations. For recipes and ideas see Chapter 9, Journey to Japan, or visit: *http://www.notmartha.org/tomake/hostesssushi/* or *http://www.vivrepourmanger.com/candy-sushi/.*

6. Watch a movie: We showed *Naruto* because we have the license to show that series and it is popular with our tweens. The tweens watched an episode while making and enjoying their candy sushi.

7. Clean up.

Materials Used

- Donated mangas from comics shop
- Manga/Anime Word Search
- Prizes: Anime DVDS, mangas (try to receive donations), anime/manga items
- Gummy worms
- Rice krispy treats
- Fruit Roll-ups
- Twizzlers
- Twinkies
- Donuts
- Licorice

Budget

$20-$60. Candy sushi and prizes were the major expense.

General Comments

Manga is really popular in teen and tween circles and this program has many possibilities, such as a Cosplay where tweens dress as their favorite characters, and other games.

SHARING THEIR FAVORITE MANGA DURING MANGA MANIA. COURTESY OF OSHAWA PUBLIC LIBRARIES GRAPHICS DEPARTMENT

Whatever Floats Your Boat

I came up with this idea after telling a tween that they can do whatever they want at a drop-in craft program and used the phrase 'Whatever floats your boat!' They said that they had never heard it before (am I really that old fashioned?!) and asked if it had something to do with root beer floats. I decided to create a program that would offer that! Basically this program can be whatever you want it to be as long as there is some kind of floats made. We've made buttons and floats, decorated bookmarks while enjoying floats, played Bingo and created floats, and watched a movie while enjoying floats – all equally as enjoyable.

Program Advertisement

Come make an awesome root beer float at the library, hangout with friends, make buttons and enjoy some cool music.

Number of Spaces Available

20

Program Preparation (1 hour)

1. Decide what kind of floats you'd like to offer. Root beer floats are a stand-by, but there are many other alternatives out there known as ice cream sodas! Options include: Black Cow, Butterbeer, Boston cooler, Snow White, and Orange Float. There's an entire Wikipedia page dedicated to it at: http://en.wikipedia.org/wiki/Ice_cream_soda

2. Once you know the sodas you'll be creating, buy the supplies or ask for donations!

3. Prepare for craft if you are offering one.

4. Pull current CDs to listen to. The 'Now That's What I Call Music' CD's are great.

5. Decide if you'd like to watch a movie and research licensing.

Room Set-up

Tables and chairs for activities and making ice cream floats

Projector and screen if showing movie

Prepare Bingo sheets if you are offering.

Program Outline

1. Icebreaker: Pick out a great icebreaker from Chapter 3. You could always have tweens state their name and their favorite ice cream flavor.

2. Describe the different kinds of floats that tweens can make and explain that there is no wrong way to make a float – even if you're lactose intolerant you can have a float (I provide coconut or soy ice cream as an alternative).

3. Play music while the tweens partake in a float free-for-all. You'll need enough ice cream, soda, cups, and any other toppings you'd like to include.

4. While the tweens are enjoying their floats they can decorate bookmarks or create a button. Our library has a fancy button-maker, but it was pretty expensive to purchase. You can also make home-made buttons a variety of ways.

5. Another alternative that tweens can do while eating floats is play a few rounds of Bingo. Everyone loves Bingo. It's always a hit! You can make your own Bingo cards using this website: http://www.dltk-cards.com/bingo/bingo1.asp

6. Watch a movie: if your library has a license to show movies, you can always show a movie or TV show while enjoying delicious floats.

7. Clean up.

Materials Used

- Different flavors of ice cream
- At least 7-8 two liters of soda (not just root beer)
- Syrups: chocolate, strawberry, butterscotch
- Other toppings can include: marshmallow fluff, gummies, licorice and more!
- Craft supplies if you'd like to do a craft
- Paper and bingo markers for bingo

Budget

$20-$60. You can do this with generic food items or donations.

General Comments

This is a very popular program and good for any age group! As you can see, there are really tons of variations so you could even offer it several times a year with very little preparation time involved.

Bling a Birdhouse

Have you heard? Bird's the word! This is a fun and simple program that fosters tons of creativity. You can find inexpensive birdhouses at many craft stores, for example, Michael's, or online at Oriental Trading Company *http://www.orientaltrading.com/design-your-own-wood-birdhouses-a2-57_6085.fltr.* You may have acrylic paint and paintbrushes on hand like we do, but this may be an additional expense. We have also hosted this program for younger children to do with their fathers for a Father's Day event.

Program Advertisement

Decorate a sweet house for birds to enjoy. Materials will be provided.

Number of Spaces Available

20

Program Preparation (1.5 hours)

1. Purchase birdhouses.

2. Purchase paint and paintbrushes, if not already available.

3. Print design ideas.

4. Cover tables with disposable tablecloths.

5. Print information on how to hang birdhouses. You can find this at: *http://www.a-home-for-wild-birds.com/bird-house-placement.html.*

Room Set-up

Tables and chairs for the craft
Cover tables with tablecloths
Cups of water, paintbrushes, and paint for each table

Program Outline

1. Icebreaker: Ask the tweens to name their favorite bird.

2. Decorate the birdhouses. A very easy program, as long as paint doesn't get everywhere.

3. Clean up.

Materials Used

- Birdhouses purchased from Michael's
- Acrylic paint
- Paintbrushes
- Handout on how to hang a birdhouse
- Handouts from Michael's on ideas for birdhouses: *http://www.michaels.com/Birdhouses/projects-craftpainting-projectype-birdhouses,default,sc.html*

Budget

$60. - $100. Birdhouses vary in price, so shop around.

General Comments

We have hosted this program several times and it always fills up. It went over well with tweens, but paint and water spilling can be bit of a problem so use low, wide containers.

Chapter 9: June

The school year is coming to an end and libraries are gearing up for another busy summer, which usually means the start of summer reading clubs. If classes are still in session, you may be hesitant to offer many programs in June, but the tweens will be disappointed if you don't! If tweens are still in school, program attendance is often greater at the beginning of June, rather than in the last few days of the month when school parties and last-minute assignments or exams are being completed. But if tweens are experiencing the first month of freedom from academics, keep June programs exciting and fun to stay in-line with the light-hearted feeling tweens have at this time of year! Nothing is more exciting than Harry Potter, a destination in Japan, and your own town's mini-version of *Jersey Shore*! If the tweens are exhausted after the end of a school year, you can also offer a relaxation night. For information on summer reading club programming, see Chapter 10: July.

Journey to Japan

As the manga and anime formats continue to rise in popularity among tweens, so does the interest in everything Japanese. Tweens are fascinated with Japanese culture, including sushi, origami, calligraphy, and crazy game shows. This program allows tweens to delve into it all without leaving the comfort of their own local library.

Program Advertisement

Do you love everything Japanese? Then come to this exciting and fun-filled program all about Japan--from Sushi to Japanese game shows, you won't want to miss this adventure!

Number of Spaces Available

20

Program Preparation (1 hour)

1. Print the Japanese translations of each tween's name (if you have advance registration).

2. Make or purchase puffed rice cereal treats.

3. Collect books about origami or print instructions from the Internet. Instructional videos are also available on YouTube for more visual learners. Origami instructions can be found at *http://www.origami-instructions.com/* and *http://www.origami-fun.com/*.

Room Set-up

Tables and chairs for calligraphy, sushi making, and origami

An open space for the relay races

Program Outline

1. Icebreaker: Choose an icebreaker from Chapter 3.

2. Japanese Calligraphy: If you have laptops or computers available for use during library programs, allow each tween to type their name into a Japanese translator website and print the results. We suggest Philip Ronan's "Your Name in Japanese" at *http://japanesetranslator.co.uk/dictionaries/your-name-in-japanese/*. If you pre-register tweens for the program, you can do this step before the program begins. Access to a computer during the program is helpful for drop-ins and in case you've made a spelling mistake. Once tweens have the print outs of the Japanese symbols for their names, they use a paint brush to paint a more artistic representation of their name.

3. Candy Sushi: Not everyone likes sushi, but almost everyone likes candy sushi! Using puffed rice cereal treats, fruit wrappers, and an assortment of gummy and/or licorice candies, teach tweens to make their own sushi rolls. You may opt to make your own rice cereal treats or to purchase pre-packaged varieties. Have plastic bags available so that tweens can take the extra sushi pieces home. Serve bever-

How to Make Candy Sushi

Ingredients
- 20 Puffed Rice treats (you can buy these pre-made or make your own)
- 20 gummy worms or Twizzlers
- 12 green-colored Fruit Roll-Ups
- 30 fish-shaped gummy candies
- Any other fun ingredients you brainstorm to stuff your sushi with!

Prepare Ingredients
- If you're working with pre-made puffed rice treats, cut the treats in half, length wise.
- Heat the treats in microwave to make them pliable. Line the treats with a gummy worm and wrap the treat around the worm like a burrito.
- Cover the rice treat/worm roll with a green fruit roll-up so it looks like seaweed.
- Put a fish on top and cover with another roll.
- If you're making your own Puffed Rice treats, you can lay your mixture out on a baking sheet covered in wax paper and work on a giant roll to cut up.
- Be creative!

Additional recipes are available online at Rachel Ray's *http://www.foodnetwork.com/recipes/sara-moulton/candy-sushi-recipe/index.html.*

ages as tweens sample their creations.

4. Origami: Origami is the traditional Japanese art of paper folding. It can vary from quite simple creations to extremely elaborate designs. Unless they are very familiar with origami, most tweens (and library staff) will be at a very beginner level. Most libraries have a variety of books about origami that include folding instructions. Choose designs that will appeal to male and female tweens. Practice folding before the program. If you have older teen volunteers, ask them to assist with this part of the program.

5. Chopstick Challenge! The Japanese are known for their crazy and hilarious game shows. A tamer, but equally fun competition is the chopstick challenge. To begin, give each tween a set of chopsticks. Demonstrate how to hold chopsticks and allow tweens the opportunity to practice their technique. Next, divide tweens into two groups for a relay race. The first person on each team will use his/her chopsticks (in one hand only) to pick up a pom pom or other small object. S/he must then carry the pom pom across the room and place it in a bowl before handing the chopsticks to the next person in line. Continue until each person has had a turn. The winner is the team that finishes first.

6. Wasabi Pea Relay: Traditional Japanese wasabi is hot, like horseradish, made from the wasabi plant, and is used in many sushi dishes. Wasabi peas, dried peas with a coating of dried wasabi, is a popular Asian snack in North America. Since wasabi is an acquired taste, allow tweens who wish to sample some peas. Once the sampling is complete, use the leftover peas for a relay race. Keeping tweens on their original teams, give each team member a drinking straw. One at a time, tweens suck on a straw until a pea sticks to the end of it. Each tween must then transport a pea to a bowl on the opposite side of the room before returning to the next person in line.

7. Award Prizes: You may wish to award books or library publicity items to the team who won the chopstick challenge and the wasabi pea relay.

8. Clean up.

Materials Used

- Computer
- Printer
- Paper (preferably construction paper or card stock)
- Paint
- Paint brushes
- Containers of water for paint brushes
- Paper towels
- Pre-packaged rice cereal treats or butter, marshmallows, puffed rice cereal, a bowl, a spoon, and a microwave to make them
- Plastic knives
- Waxed paper

- Gummy candies (worms, fish, berries, Swedish fish, etc.)
- Licorice
- Fruit wrappers
- Plates
- Napkins
- Beverages and cups
- Origami paper
- Scissors
- Chopsticks
- Pom poms or other small objects
- Bowls
- Drinking straws
- Wasabi peas

Budget

Approximately $40. Food adds an additional expense. Ask your local Chinese or Japanese restaurant to donate chopsticks, or ask library staff to bring their own from home.

General Comments

This was a program of highs and lows. The chopstick relay challenge was a huge hit! In fact, most tweens wanted additional laps of the race. Candy sushi and learning Japanese calligraphy were also extremely popular. While most tweens enjoyed the origami, several did get frustrated; especially the big tweens (us!) running the program. We incorrectly assumed that paper folding would be easy to do. Thank you to tweens Cindy and Claire for teaching us a thing or two about origami!

Harry Potter Potions

Even though more than fifteen years have passed since J.K. Rowling's first Harry Potter book hit the shelves, Harry Potter mania is still very much alive and hopefully always will be. Although this program was originally created to coincide with the release of a Harry Potter movie, it can be offered at any time of year. Because its elements include a variety of potions and concoctions, it can be easily tweaked to fit any magic or science themed events that you wish to host. Put on your Harry Potter costume and enjoy this program!

Program Advertisement

The Harry Potter books and movies may be complete, but we still want to celebrate! Make some spectacular potions and crafts … Harry Potter style!

Number of Spaces Available

20

Program Preparation (1 hour)

1. Make ice cubes, mix food coloring into the water. You will need 2 ice cubes per tween.

2. Create labels for each food and drink potion, listing only the potion name.

3. Print Hedwig Droppings gift tags, available online at *https://sites.google.com/site/thetweenscene/*; and *http://www.budget101.com/harrypotter/id757.htm.*

Room Set-up

Tables and chairs for all activities

Two designated tables for food and drink potions

Program Outline

1. Icebreaker: Ask each tween to state his/her name and favorite Harry Potter book, character, or movie.

2. Ice Charm Spell: Give each tween two glasses. One should be filled ¾ full of water, the other ¾ full of rubbing alcohol. Make it very clear that tweens are not to drink either of the glasses of liquid. The last thing you want is to call poison control because someone drank the rubbing alcohol! Give each tween two colored ice cubes, one for each glass. Before letting tweens drop the ice cubes in the glasses, ask them what they think will happen. Afterwards, explain that ice will float in water because the water has a higher density than the ice. (One way to think about density is how thick and heavy something is.) Rubbing alcohol has a lower density than either the ice or the water. When you place an ice cube in rubbing alcohol it will drop to the bottom. Because the rubbing alcohol is less dense than the ice or the water, the alcohol will float on top of the water. This charm is also available at *http://www.budget101.com/harry-potter/ice-charm-821.html.*

3. Breathing Fungus Spell: Here's everyone's chance to capture fungus breath! Since this spell is best done in groups rather than individually, give each group (up to five tweens in a group) a glass bottle, a package of dried yeast, 1 teaspoon of sugar, a balloon, a rubber band, and a bowl. To begin, one group member pours warm water into a bottle and swishes it around. After discarding the water, another group member adds the yeast to the bottle, and another adds the sugar and swirls. Another

---

Food and Drink Potions

Sleeping Potion – blue drink mix

Extract of Pituitary – lemonade

Dragon tears – red drink mix

Excitability Formula – orange drink mix

Hippogriff Gizzard – gelatin or jelly

Bloodworms – gummy worms

Gnome Boogies – chocolate chips

Yeti Fur - coconut

Fire Ants - red sprinkles

Pond Ooze - jam

Additional potion ingredients are available online at "Harry Potter Party Games" at *http://www.purpletrail.com/partytrail/general-parties/magic_theme/harry-potter-party-games.*

"I hear you've been bad
And that's the scoop...
So today you can have
some of
Hedwig's Poop"

"I hear you've been bad
And that's the scoop...
So today you can have
some of
Hedwig's Poop"

"I hear you've been bad
And that's the scoop...
So today you can have
some of
Hedwig's Poop"

"I hear you've been bad
And that's the scoop...
So today you can have
some of
Hedwig's Poop"

"I hear you've been bad
And that's the scoop...
So today you can have
some of
Hedwig's Poop"

"I hear you've been bad
And that's the scoop...
So today you can have
some of
Hedwig's Poop"

"I hear you've been bad
And that's the scoop...
So today you can have
some of
Hedwig's Poop"

"I hear you've been bad
And that's the scoop...
So today you can have
some of
Hedwig's Poop"

"I hear you've been bad
And that's the scoop...
So today you can have
some of
Hedwig's Poop"

member adds ½ cup of warm water and swirls. Yet another member covers the neck of the bottle with a balloon and secures it with a rubber band and places the bottle in a bowl of warm water. Ask the tweens why they think the balloon inflated on its own. Explain that yeast is alive. It is made of living cells. Yeast is a fungus, just like mushrooms. We use yeast to bake bread. In addition to the beauty of mushrooms, fungi provide a critical part of nature's continuous rebirth: fungi recycle dead organic matter into useful nutrients. When you add the warm water, the yeast feeds on the sugar. As it feeds, it breathes. Yeast breathes out carbon dioxide which fills the balloon. You have now captured yeast breath! This spell is also available online at *http://www.budget101.com/harry-potter/breathing-fungus-spell-827.html.*

4. Invisible Ink Spell: Give each tween a piece of white paper and a white crayon to write a message. Remind tweens to press hard with the crayon, otherwise the spell won't work. After everyone has written a message, each tween must pass their paper to another tween. Tweens brush black paint over the piece of paper to reveal a message.

5. Food and Drink Potions: Now that everyone has worked up an appetite, it's time to create some edible potions! Direct tweens to the potion tables, where items should be properly displayed and labeled. Have one table for food potions and another for drink potions. Give each tween a cup and allow them to add any of the drink ingredients, concocting their own original potion. After they make their drinks, give each tween a bowl and allow them to make an ice cream potion.

6. Hedwig Droppings: End this program with an edible craft … Hedwig droppings. Give each tween a small plastic bag that they can fill with chocolate covered raisins. Affix the witty gift card with ribbon for "owl poop!"

7. Award Prizes: You may wish to have a Harry Potter book available as a door prize.

8. Clean up.

Materials Used

- Ice cube trays
- Food coloring
- Tap water
- Glasses (two per tween)
- Rubbing alcohol
- Glass bottles (one per group)
- Packets of yeast
- Sugar
- Balloons
- Rubber bands
- Bowls
- White paper
- White crayons
- Black paint

- Paintbrushes
- Blue drink mix
- Lemonade
- Red drink mix
- Orange drink mix
- Gelatin or jelly
- Gummy worms
- Ice cream
- Chocolate chips
- Coconut
- Red sprinkles
- Jam
- Bowls
- Spoons
- Cups
- Small plastic bags
- Ribbon
- Chocolate covered raisins
- Cardstock for food and drink labels

Budget

Approximately $50 for yeast, rubbing alcohol, ice cream, and drinks. Most of the toppings for the food and drink potions for our program were leftover from other food-based programs. Otherwise, these may be an additional expense.

General Comments

Unless you have a freezer in your programming space, begin with the Ice Charm Spell so that the ice cubes don't melt. Having student volunteers or extra staff on hand will make this program run smoothly. Because there are so many different activities that all require tables, it is helpful to enlist help to clear tables and clean up as you go. Getting the balloon over the top of the bottle in the Fungus Spell can also be difficult for younger tweens, so they may need assistance. Don't be surprised if the tweens want you to sample their food and drink potions!

Oshawa Shore

Okay, okay, we admit, this is one of our more controversial programs. But this is one that the tweens asked for--they begged us to do a *Jersey Shore* themed program. Maybe we also have a bit of an affinity for Jersey Shore and, ahem, Pauly D. Whether you're a Snooki lover or hater, this program is easy and fun to do!

Program Advertisement

It's T-Shirt Time! Here's the situation--the Oshawa Public Library (insert your library) is bringing Jersey to town, Oshawa style! No, we're not showing the TV Show, we will be hosting a fun evening with a library spin of GTL, a dance-off, and more. Even if you don't know what *Jersey Shore* is, this is a fun party for you!

Number of Spaces Available

20

Program Preparation (1 hour)

1. Watch an episode of *Jersey Shore* if you're not familiar with the series.

2. Print/create enough handouts for each tween: *Jersey Shore* Madlib and create your *Jersey Shore* name. If you are familiar with the television show, every guido and guidette has a nickname! Snooki, J-WOWW, The Situation, Paul D, Ronnie, Sammi Sweetheart, and Vinny all have cool nicknames. We created a handout that helps tweens decide on their names. We arbitrarily came up with a system of adding a Y or I to their first name and then matching their favourite number with a corresponding random word such as Dancer, Attitude, Angel, Show, Shark, etc. An example following this formula that we created would be: Tiffi Attitude. Cabs are hee-yah!

3. Tweens love madlibs! The sillier, the better. We created a madlib and began by explaining what nouns, adjectives, and verbs are and what a madlib is. Then we asked tweens to fill in the blanks and read the hilarious story aloud! The tweens wanted to do it again by filling in different words.

4. Collect books about pop culture, biographies on the characters, or books on the state of New Jersey.

Jersey Shore Mad Lib

Pauly D: Sad thing is like he'll be _____ (verb) with _____ (name #1, girl) tomorrow.

Vinny: I _____ (verb). How does she just like do that to _____ (name #2)?

Pauly D: I _____ (verb), after they just _____ (verb). What do we do? Should we _____ (verb) _____ (name #1)?

Vinny: Wait, I _____ (verb) and _____ (noun). Why don't we (verb) _____an _____ (adjective) _____ (noun).

Pauly D: Yea, oh my _____ (noun), let's do it. We'll _____ (verb) it so they don't even think it's us. We'll _____ (verb) it _____ (adjective) _____ (adjective) so bring a _____ (noun). Dear _____ (name #1), _____ (name #2) _____ (verb) with _____ (name #3) in the _____ (noun).

Vinny: If ya know what I mean.

Pauly D: If ya know what I mean.

Vinny: Don't _____ (verb) her we _____ (verb) it.

Pauly D: Oh I won't _____ (verb) her bro but she needs to know it's _____ (adjective) _____ (noun).

Here's a hint!

Noun- is a peson, place, or thing. Ex: boy, girl, home, lake, telephone, car.

Adjective- is a describing word. Ex: Tall, cold, big.

Verb- is an action word, or an "ing" word. Ex: jumping, hopping, skipping, sleeping

Make Your Own Jersey Shore Nickname!

Snooki, J-WOWW, Mike The Situation, Pauly D, Ronnie, Sammi Sweetheart, and Vinny all have cool nicknames. Why not create one of your own? Here are some suggestions on how to come up with a Jersey Shore worthy name.

YOU CAN...

1) **Add a Y or I**

   Ex. Nick -> Nicky
   Ann -> Anni

   OR

   Add an IE

   Ex. Chris -> Chrisie
   Robin -> Robie

   OR **Go By Your First Name and Last Initial**

   Ex. Christopher Robin -> Chris R
   Harry Potter -> Harry P

**Write down your name
thus far HERE:**

_____

2) **Create A Nickname**

   Pick Two Numbers Between 1-9
   Feel free to pick the same number twice!

   Write them HERE: _____   _____

   Then Flip the Page!

Make Your Own Jersey Shore Nickname!

2) Create A Nickname

Find the words that correspond to the two numbers you picked in the columns below, then copy out your new nickname!

Column One	Column Two
The	Attitude
Big	Twist
Crazy	Angel
Wild	Child
Sweet	Party
Loud	Hawk
Reckless	Dancer
Fabulous	Show
Real	Shark

Write them HERE: _____ _____

Now put Part One and Part Two together to read your Jersey Shore name!

_____

5. For more *Jersey Shore* information visit: *http://en.wikipedia.org/wiki/Jersey_Shore_(TV_series)*.

Room Set-up

Tables and chairs for handouts

An open space for the relay races and 'Beat the Beat' dance off

Program Outline

1. Icebreaker: Choose an icebreaker from Chapter 3.

2. Find out your *Jersey Shore* name.

3. Beat the Beat Dance-Off: One of the best parts of the Shore is the dance scene. The cast mates love to dance and have great moves, including the fist pump. Play some upbeat techno music and organize the competition however you want--call out dance moves, turn it into musical chairs, give them glow sticks, and tap them on the shoulder until the best dancer is left standing.

4. Jersey Shore Madlib.

5. GTL Relay Race: In the *Jersey Shore* world, GTL stands for Gym, Tan, and Laundry, baby! It's what every guido needs in his life in order to survive. This relay starts with five pound weights that the tweens have to pump ten times, and then they have to color in Snooki's tan as fast as they can, and finally they have to fold five shirts. It's a tough life! To have tweens color in Snooki's tan, you can print out a picture of Snooki in black and white and give the tweens a brown crayon. An outline image can be found at *http://how.to-draw.co.uk/?s=Snooki*.

6. Award Prizes: You may wish to award prizes to the team who won the GTL Relay Race. Glowsticks make excellent, inexpensive prizes and are available at most dollar stores.

7. Clean up.

Materials Used

- Computer
- Printer
- Paper (preferably construction paper or card stock)
- Weights
- Brown crayons
- Techno music
- Glowsticks
- T-shirts to fold

Budget

This program is cheap. Most if it is made up of hand-outs created in-house,and the only expense would be prizes if you decide to have any.

General Comments

Even though *Jersey Shore* is no longer in production, we thought it would be good to include. Not only does it demonstrate how a pop culture trend can be adapted to the library environment, but it also illustrates "outside of the box" programming ideas. You know the climate of your community and whether or not a program such as this would go over well.

Spa Night

This program has run under a few titles: Spa Night, Relaxation Night, DIY Spa Essentials for Teens, and Lotions and Potions. It's all the same thing – making different bath/personal products yourself! In the past we have made lip balm, bath bombs, body scrub, body glitter, and more. Of course, this appeals more to tween girls but we have had the occasional dude stop in to learn about the powers of exfoliation.

Program Advertisement

Whether you are making it for yourself or as a gift, this is a programme that you won't want to miss! You will get a chance to make your own lip balm, bath bomb and body scrub! Use your imagination to mix scents and colours to create your own at-home spa! Get creative

Number of Spaces Available

20

Program Preparation (1-2 hours)

1. Decide what spa items you will be offering. If you search 'DIY Spa' or 'Homemade bath products' online you will find lots of results! We will include recipes for lip balm, bath bomb, body scrub, and body glitter.

2. Purchase items needed.

3. Collect books about beauty or spa items.

Room Set-up

Tables and chairs for different stations. We usually run only 3 stations as that's what we have time for.

Program Outline

1. Icebreaker: Choose an icebreaker from Chapter 3. Have everyone introduce themselves. Explain what you will be doing and how the program is set up. We usually have three stations and a different spa item to make at each station.

2. Body Scrub: This will likely take the least amount of time out of all the stations listed.
    Exfoliating Body Scrub
    Ingredients:
    -   Salt or sugar
    -   Oil
    -   Scents

    Mix 2 parts Salt with one part Oil and add scents. Enjoy!

3. Have small bowls set out for mixing and containers for finished product.

4. Lip balm: We usually do cocoa flavor because who doesn't like chocolate? You can even add cocoa powder for extra chocolatey goodness.

    Cocoa Butter Lip Balm
    Ingredients:
    -   Cocoa Butter
    -   Scents
    -   Colour

    Mix cocoa butter with a small amount of scent and colour.

    Another way of doing this is to use beeswax and vitamin E. You'll need a microwave to heat up the three, then you add whatever scent you'd like. You'll also need a container.

5. Bath Bomb: This will take the longest of the listed activities. The tweens can pack the bath bomb with their hands, or use candy molds.

    Bath Bomb
    Ingredients:
    ½ cup Citric Acid
    1 cup Baking Soda
    ¾ cup Corn Starch
    ¼ cup Sugar
    About 5-6 drops Food Colouring
    Essential Oils

    Mix all dry ingredients together. Add essential oils 1 drop at a time.

    Using a spray bottle, spray a mixture of water and food coloring into the dry mixture until damp.

    Form into balls.

    Let dry for 24 hours.   You'll need wax paper or plastic wrap for the tweens to take home. This recipe makes about 12 bombs.

6. Body Glitter: This is the easiest station. You'll need a small container for the body glitter. All the tweens need to do is put the aloe vera in their small container and add loose glitter and mix! You can also add a scent if you'd like as well, we find vanilla to be particularly popular.

7. Clean up.

Materials Used

- Computer
- Printer
- Beeswax
- Olive Oil
- Vitamin E oil capsules
- Scents (vanilla extract, cocoa powder, lavender oil, etc)
- Color (food coloring)
- Microwave
- Small/medium sealable containers for storing the finished product
- Salt and sugar (sugar is finer and will be more gentle on sensitive skin)
- Oil (olive, vegetable etc)
- ½ cup citric acid
- 1 cup baking soda
- ¾ cup corn starch
- ¼ cup sugar or Epsom salts
- Food colouring
- Aloe Vera
- Glitter
- Spray bottle
- Wax paper or plastic wrap

Budget

Approximately $40. You can get many items from the dollar store or ask your colleagues if they have any products to donate.

General Comments

This program has endless possibilities. Depending on the materials you have available, you can make sleep masks, body butter, masks, lotion, cuticle cream, and more! As mentioned before, this does appeal more to the ladies of the group but you can always try a manly approach as well with DIY deodorant.

HANGING OUT AFTER A DAY AT THE "LIBRARY SPA!". COURTESY OF OSHAWA PUBLIC LIBRARIES GRAPHICS DEPARTMENT

Chapter 10: July

Summer is here...are you ready for it? Students are out of school and the library is about to become a hub-bub of excitement and activity! While there are still collections to be maintained, outreach events to attend, and monthly reports to be written, programming definitely jumps to the forefront for all library staff in July. During the summer months, most libraries participate in state-wide or national reading clubs which usually follow a theme. These themes can be as broad as the entire genre of fantasy, or as specific as dinosaurs. Use your imagination and try to stretch the limits of each theme. In previous years, the Canadian Toronto Dominion Bank® Summer Reading Club chose the themes of "Agent 009" and "Destination Jungle," which strongly influenced the following program outlines for July and August. As you can see, the thematic limits have been stretched to include video games, scavenger hunts, space travel and photography!

Evidence Hunter

This program gives tweens the opportunity to learn about the physical orientation of the library while putting their investigative skills to the test! Each team receives a disposable camera and is given a list of ten clues/tasks to complete. Library staff then takes the cameras/evidence for "processing" and announce the team with the most correct photos as the winners! In case teams finish before the allotted time is up, there are five bonus clues to find and photograph.

Program Advertisement

Help us solve a mystery at the library with photo evidence! Come prepared to follow clues and hunt around the entire library branch.

Number of Spaces Available

30

Program Preparation (1 hour)

1. Purchase disposable cameras (one per team).

2. Re-write the following scenario and clues to reflect the layout and features of your library. Alter the order of each team's clues so not all tweens are in the same area at once. An editable copy is available online at *https://sites.google.com/site/thetweenscene/home/july*.

The Crime Scene

At approximately 3 a.m. last night, a male suspect entered the library through the auditorium ramp doors. The alarm was not triggered, so the suspect had a lot of time to search the premises looking for valuable books and money. He left behind a trail of evidence. Police are asking for your help to photograph the evidence so that it can be sent away for processing.

Police Procedures

*   Stay inside the library and take all of the photos with your team.
*   *Everyone* on the team, except the photographer, *must* be in the photo somewhere.
*   Share the camera so everyone gets to be the photographer at one of the sites.
*   Do not disturb other library customers or make a lot of noise.
*   Use a numbered Post-it somewhere in the photo to show which challenge you're doing.
*   You have 1 hour to complete the first 10 tasks.
*   If you finish early, return to the auditorium to see if police have found additional clues for you to process.

CLUES

1. The thief accidentally walked through the bushes before entering the library and left clue in the hardcover teen fiction section.
2. While in the hardcover teen fiction section, balance books on your heads. Try VERY HARD not to drop them.
3. The thief lost part of his disguise when he tripped on the magazine shelving in the adult department. Can you find the disguise?
4. While in the adult department, combine two or more book/magazine/movie/CD titles to make a funny or interesting sentence.
5. The thief left this clue behind when he decided to take a break and get a coffee at the public coffee cart in the fiction section!
6. While you are in the adult fiction section, act out the picture on the cover of a book, and have someone hold the book so the police can compare.
7. The thief was upset when he realized that the basement bathrooms were locked. He was so mad that he left another clue behind.
8. The thief was going to use this to carry his stolen goods but lost it under one of the tables in the Story Hour Room.

9. Act out a scene from a traditional fairy tale or folk tale – try to find the book in the Story Hour Room and include it in your photo.

10. I don't know how it got there, but the photocopier is wearing a part of the thief's disguise!

Additional Clues

11. Find a scary book in the children's department and give us your best scared looks.

12. Find the funniest book/CD/movie title you can, show the cover and the team laughing.

13. The thief left this clue behind in the children's/family DVD section.

14. Find a children's/family movie you know and act out a scene from it (get the cover in the photo!)

15. Do a cool photo – your choice.

3. Create and/or gather the clues. Hide them just before the program starts and remind library staff not to remove them. You can create fingerprints by looking for a fingerprint online, as well as a footprint. Or, if you are artistic, you can sketch them yourself. An online image of a great fingerprint is available at: *http://www.vetmed.vt.edu/education/ curriculum/vm8054/labs/lab14/IMAGES/FINGERPRINT.jpg*.

Clue Answers
1. leaf
3. sunglasses
5. fingerprint
7. newspaper
8. piece of fabric
10. hat
13. footprint

Room Set-up

Clues are hidden throughout the library requiring minimal room set-up.

Program Outline

1. Icebreaker: Ask tweens to state their name, and the name of their favorite detective novel, movie, or television show.

2. Formation of Teams: Divide tweens into 10 teams of 3, or 6 teams of 5.

3. Camera Time! Open a camera and assign it to a team. Write the team number on each camera and all team members' names and contact information on a separate piece of paper, as you will need to contact them once evidence comes back from processing.

4. Setting the Scene: Read aloud and distribute the crime scene story and police procedures. Give each team a stack of Post-it notes and a marker, as teams need to include the number of each clue they are capturing in each photo.

5. Distribute the Clues: Give each team a copy of the clues.

6. Collect and Process the Evidence: Once all tweens have collected the evidence, they must return their cameras to library staff for processing. Tell tweens how long the processing will take and give an approximate date of when you will be in contact with them to announce the winner. When you take the cameras to be developed, ask the photo lab employee to write the team number from each undeveloped camera on the outside of each developed photo package. This way you will easily be able to keep track of teams.

7. Determine a Winner and Award Prizes: Check each photo to ensure that the answer is correct, that tweens have taken turns behind the camera, and that the remaining tweens are in the photos. Bonus photos can be used as tie-breakers or as bonus points, making for a possible score of 15/10. If there are multiple winners, consider offering multiple prizes or drawing one in a lottery. Contact the members of the winning team and arrange for prize pick-up. Contact the remaining teams and offer them copies of the photos, or post them online if photo release forms have been filed.

8. Clean up.

Materials Used

- Disposable cameras
- Marker
- Pen and piece of paper
- Post-it notes
- Markers
- Leaf
- Sunglasses
- Fingerprint
- Newspaper
- Piece of fabric
- Hat
- Footprint

Budget

Approximately $75 for disposable cameras and $20 to have the film developed.

General Comments

Since it can be expensive to purchase and develop so many disposable cameras, you may want to ask tweens to bring their own digital camera or cell phone camera. After the program is done, tweens can email the pictures to you for judging purposes. Be sure to set a strict deadline for submissions. If a library computer is available, tweens can download their photos before leaving the program. If you choose to use disposable cameras, consider putting more tweens on each team to limit costs. Open cameras as you assign them to a team, so that any unopened cameras can be returned.

Journey through the Jungle

Here is another terrific program that combines the use of library resources, trivia, and a scavenger hunt. While this outline focuses specifically on a jungle theme, it can be adapted to almost any theme or topic. The only limit is your imagination!

Program Advertisement

Never been to the jungle before? Now's your chance to answer wild clues and compete for prizes through the jungle that is the library!

Number of Spaces Available

20

Program Preparation (1 hour)

1. Pull a variety of jungle animal books from the collection for Jungle True or False. Or, if you prefer, the tweens can use the library catalogue to find titles.

2. Rewrite and print the scavenger hunt clue cards to reflect your collection and physical space. Hide clues prior to the program. Remind staff that clues should not be removed.

3. If there's time left over, tweens can do the jungle word scramble. See reproducible.

4. Transfer the Jungle Jeopardy questions and answers to a Microsoft® PowerPoint presentation or physical game board. Questions are also available online courtesy of TD Summer Reading Club, developed by Toronto Public Library in partnership with Library and Archives Canada, sponsored by TD Bank Group. *http://www.collectionscanada.gc.ca/obj/009003/f2/009003-10-1000-e.pdf*, pages 76-78.

The anaconda is a huge type of snake that lives in the jungles of South America. Anacondas can be up to:

a) **9 meters long**

b) 15 meters long

c) 17 meters long

Animals 100 points

Scavenger Hunt Clue Cards

1. Visiting the JUNGLE is quite a risk; find an encyclopedia to see what you're dealing with. There's a paper in the JUNGLE you must grab, but if you don't put the book back, that would be bad.

2. Seventeen, Say What?, J14, it's a jungle over in the teen magazines.

3. The water is murky, danger is near, piranhas and fake turtles are what you must fear. Safari life is tougher than you think, go to the story hour room and get yourself a drink!

4. This one's for a true book lover: Find a book with a jungle on the cover. (Show it to your tour guide)

5. Back to the beginning you must go, your very best Tarzan call you must show.

6. If jungle books are what you seek, open the binder and take a peek.

7. In the jungle you must stay, until the dice rolls 5 or 8!

Poison arrow frogs warn predators that they are poisonous to eat by:
    a) biting them back
    b) **being brightly colored**
    c) having a very distinctive croak
    Animals 200 points

A Macaw is:
    a) **a type of parrot**
    b) a type of small monkey
    c) a type of brightly colored fish
    Animals 300 points

About what percentage of the world's insects live in the rainforest?
    a) 65%
    b) **80%**
    c) 90%
    Animals 400 points

A Pangolin is a very curious mammal. It is notable for:
    a) **having scales like a snake**
    b) laying eggs like a bird
    c) being able to howl at 50 decibels
    Animals 500 points

A liana is:
    a) a small monkey
    b) **a type of vine**
    c) a South American dance
    Plants 100 points

The world's largest flower, the Raffelesia, grows in the jungles of Indonesia. The Raffelesia is also notable for:
    a) tasting like chocolate
    b) having purple, polka-dotted petals
    c) **smelling like rotten meat**
    Plants 200 points

Rubber is one of many products from the jungle. Rubber comes from:
    a) **tree sap**
    b) ant eggs
    c) dried leaves
    Plants 300 points

A Mangrove is a tree that is distinctive for:
　　a) having enormous, waxy circular leaves
　　b) **supporting itself on roots that look like stilts**
　　c) being the world's only carnivorous tree
Plants 400 points

Which of these products does not come from a jungle plant?
　　a) coffee
　　b) chocolate
　　c) **plastic**
Plants 500 points

The world's largest river is:
　　a) the Nile
　　b) the Mississipi
　　c) **the Amazon**
Water 100 points

The Amazon rivers flows through this country:
　　a) Bhutan
　　b) **Brazil**
　　c) Borneo
Water 200 points

A ____ is a type of heavy rainstorm that occurs in the tropics.
　　a) **monsoon**
　　b) mangrove
　　c) manatee
Water 300 points

The Amazon river is so big that in some places it stretches this far from bank to bank:
　　a) 3 km
　　b) 7.5 km
　　c) **10km**
Water 400 points

The highest recorded rainfall in the world took place in a rainforest in India. More than ___ meters of rain fell in a single year!
　　a) 17m
　　b) **26m**
　　c) 38m
Water 500 points

Which Continent has no rainforests?
  a) Africa
  b) **Europe**
  c) North America
  Geography 100 points

The rainforest in Brazil is called the:
  a) **Amazon**
  b) Arawak
  c) Anaconda
  Geography 200 points

Most of the world's rainforests are found:
  a) in the Tropic of Cancer
  b) in the Tropic of Capricorn
  c) **around the Equator**
  Geography 300 points

Rainforests are being cut down at an alarming rate. Some experts estimate rainforests are being cut down at a rate of:
  a) 25 football fields a week
  b) 25 football fields a day
  c) **25 football fields a minute**
  Geography 400 points

Life in the rainforest is incredibly diverse. Despite only covering about 7% of the world's surface, rainforests contain:
  a) about a quarter of the world's known species
  b) **about half of the world's known species**
  c) about two thirds of the world's known species
  Geography 500 points

Room Set-up

Tables and chairs for Jungle Jeopardy

Program Outline

1. Icebreaker: Ask tweens to state their name, and their favorite jungle (or non-jungle) animal.

2. Formation of Teams: Divide tweens into pairs/groups of two. If there are uneven numbers, you can have one team of three.

3. Jungle True or False: Similar to the icebreaker "Two Truths and a Lie," this game challenges tweens to research their favorite animal and come up with two correct and one incorrect fact to share with the group. Other teams must then guess which of the statements is false.

Jungle True or False
(Target Audience: Ages 9–12)

Approximate Time: 30 to 45 minutes

Introduction:
In this game, teams of children will attempt to pick out the false "fact" about different jungle animals.

Materials:
- non-fiction books about jungle animals at a range of different reading levels (preferably with lots of fun facts!).
- pencils or pens
- scrap paper (at least one small piece per person

Instructions:
1. Divide the children into teams of 3 members.
2. Each team must find a book about an animal that they are interested in. Give each team 10 to 15 minutes to use their book to come up with three sets of three "facts" about their animal. Each set of facts should have two true facts and one false fact (e.g., "tigers are orange and black", "tigers only eat bananas", "tigers live in India"). Be prepared to give examples to the groups.
3. When each team has prepared three sets of facts, the teams take turns presenting their facts. The other teams then vote on which "fact" is false. Teams take turns presenting their facts, until all teams have presented all three sets of facts. Teams can sit in a big circle if there's space, and present one set of facts at a time. Alternately, teams can take turns coming to the front of the group and present their three sets of facts all at once.

ALSO AVAILABLE ONLINE COURTESY OF TD SUMMER READING CLUB, DEVELOPED BY TORONTO PUBLIC LIBRARY IN PARTNERSHIP WITH LIBRARY AND ARCHIVES CANADA, SPONSORED BY TD BANK GROUP. *HTTP://WWW.COLLECTIONS CANADA.GC.CA/OBJ/009003/F2/009003-10-1000-E.PDF*, PAGE 93.

4. Scavenger Hunt: Give teams the first scavenger hunt clue, which will lead them throughout the library until the tasks are complete.

5. Jungle Jeopardy: If there is time after the scavenger hunt, play a game of Jungle Jeopardy using either a physical game board or a Microsoft® PowerPoint presentation.

6. Award prizes, if available.

7. Clean up.

Jungle Jeopardy
(Target Audience: Ages 6–8 or 9–12)

Approximate time: 45 minutes

Introduction:
This is a team activity in which participants test their knowledge of jungle facts and trivia.

Materials:
- A large display surface (a blank wall, whiteboard or chalkboard)
- 20 to 25 large blank cards
- Markers
- Non-fiction books about jungles and rainforests
- 1 pair of dice

Instructions:
1. Before the program begins, find 5 questions on 4 to 5 jungle/rainforest topics (for a total of 20 to 25 questions). Alternately, use the questions below (note: the correct answers are in **bold**). You may want to come up with several sets of questions, in case there is time for multiple rounds of the game.
2. Write the questions on pieces of card, and arrange on the display surface face down as on the television show "Jeopardy"; by subject (vertical rows) and difficulty (horizontal columns). Points ranging from 100 to 500 are assigned to each question, with 100 points awarded for correctly answering the easiest question, 200 for the second easiest, etc.
3. Form children into teams of 4 or 5, and give them a few minutes to choose a fun jungle name for their team.
4. Each team then rolls the two dice to pick who goes first.
5. The teams try to guess the correct answers to questions about the chosen jungle topics. If correct, the team is awarded the number of points card is worth. If incorrect, card remains in play and the next team gets to choose a question to answer.
6. You should decide in advance whether teams can answer multiple questions per round. Base this decision on the number of children participating, and the potential for all teams to get to answer a set of questions.

Materials Used

- Books about jungle animals
- Paper and pencils
- Scavenger hunt clue cards
- Laptop, projector, screen and Microsoft® PowerPoint presentation or physical game board
- White boards, erasable markers
- Prizes

Budget

$0-$40 depending on the prizes offered

General Comments

Tweens never seem to get bored with scavenger hunts! Not only do scavenger hunts incorporate the collection and physical orientation of the library, but they also have a very minimal or even no expense. This makes them the perfect fit for most libraries!

Jungle Boogie Band Hero Tournament

For many tweens, videogaming is an integral part of everyday life. While some tweens have their own videogame systems at home, some do not. Even if they do own a system, it is always more fun to play on the big screen and with friends. Wouldn't you want to show off your gaming skills if you were an awesome player?! This program focuses on the game Band Hero®, which is available for most game consoles. Rock Band® is another music game that could be used. Note that special equipment (drums, guitars, and a microphone) is required for band video games. Instruments can either be purchased separately or as a kit with the video game.

Program Advertisement

Are you ready to rock? Compete for bragging rights and prizes in our Band Hero Tournament. Participants are welcome to enter with a full band (drummer, vocals, bass, and lead guitar), but this is not necessary.

Number of Spaces Available

20

Program Preparation (15-30 minutes)

1. Purchase or borrow a video game system (Wii, PlayStation, or Xbox 360) if you do not already own one.

2. Print tournament brackets so that a winner can be determined. Free bracket generators are available online at Print Your Brackets, *http://www.printyourbrackets.com/*.

3. Print a list of songs available on the game so that tweens can easily make their selections.

4. Practice using the game and setting up the equipment, or find someone who is familiar with the process.

5. Transfer the Music Jeopardy questions and answers to a Microsoft® PowerPoint presentation or physical game board. A Microsoft® PowerPoint presentation at *https://sites.google.com/site/thetweenscene/* is available online.

6. Print copies of the Jungle Word Scramble.

JUNGLE Word Scramble

Can you figure out the words from the mixed-up letters below?

1) Isevn

2) Epatelhn

3) Ochoreines

4) Dkraaav

5) Eethach

6) Ntrepah

7) Dheeghgo

8) Lokaa Earb

9) Hairpna

10) Lrume

11) Rvtleu

12) Dymtiuih

13) Tpuosahpomip

14) Onauct

15) Elbeste

16) Oegnosmo

17) Shmto

18) Ueltrt

19) Glilaorat

20) Dticnepee

These sample questions may need to be updated to reflect current musical trends and tween heart throbs.

Which of the following is the theme song of "The Hills"?
- Living in the City
- Umbrella
- **Unwritten**
- Paparazzi

  Songs and Albums – 10 points

Which of the following was Katy Perry's second single?
- I Kissed a Girl
- Waking Up in Vegas
- Thinking of You
- **Hot N' Cold**

  Songs and Albums – 20 points

What was Rihanna's first single?
- **Pon de Replay**
- Disturbia
- SOS
- Unfaithful

  Songs and Albums – 30 points

The Michael Buble song "Haven't Met You Yet" is off of which of his albums?
- It's Time
- The Best is Yet to Come
- **Crazy Love**
- Call Me Irresponsible

  Songs and Albums – 40 points

Which of these albums is the highest earning of all time?
- **Thriller (Michael Jackson)**
- Dark Side of the Moon (Pink Floyd)
- Back in Black (AC/DC)
- Bat Out of Hell (Meat Loaf)

  Songs and Albums – 50 points

In what song do these lyrics appear: "'Cause you were Romeo, I was a scarlet letter, And my daddy said stay away from Juliet"?
- **Love Story**
- Like Romeo and Juliet
- Fairytale
- Written in the Stars

  Lyrics – 10 points

In what song do the following lyrics appear: "I wanna hold em' like they do in Texas Plays / Fold em' let em' hit me raise it baby stay with me"
- The Game
- **Poker Face**
- Bad Romance
- If You Can Afford Me
Lyrics– 20 points

In what song do these lyrics appear: "You gave my life direction / a game show love connection"
- Airplanes
- **Hey Soul Sister**
- Rock That Body
- The Way You Are
Lyrics– 30 points

Miley Cyrus can't wait…
- **To see you again.**
- To be near you again.
- To talk to you again.
- To dance with you again.
Lyrics– 40 points

Which of the following is NOT a name in Lady Gaga's "Alejandro"?
- Fernando
- Roberto
- Alejandro
- **Bernardo**
Lyrics– 50 points

How many notes are in an octave?
- 2
- 5
- **8**
- 10
Musical Fun Facts– 10 points

A Gibson is a type of…
- Drum set
- Amp
- Microphone
- **Guitar**
Musical Fun Facts– 20 points

Which of the following is not a real instrument?

- Géophone
- Didgeridoo
- Gemshorn
- **Aushount**

  Musical Fun Facts– 30 points

How many strings does the standard guitar have?

- 4
- 5
- **6**
- 7

  Musical Fun Facts– 40 points

What are 8-Tracks?

- Instrumental backings that singers use when recording their songs.
- **A way of listening to music before tapes or CDs.**
- CDs that have exactly 8 tracks.
- Songs that use 8 or more instruments.

  Musical Fun Facts– 50 points

The Movie "Bandslam" featured which star of the film High School Musical?

- Ashley Tisdale
- **Vanessa Hudgins**
- Zac Effron
- Lucas Grabeel

  Music and the Movies– 10 points

Taylor Swift's "Today was a Fairytale" was on the soundtrack of which recent romantic comedy?

- Leap Year
- She's out of my League
- When in Rome
- **Valentine's Day**

  Music and the Movies– 20 points

In "Nick and Norah's Infinite Playlist", what band are they trying to hunt down?

- **Where's Fluffy?**
- The Pink Pajamas
- Long Night
- The Smashers

  Music and the Movies– 30 points

Which of the following actresses/singers has NOT released an album?
- Ashley Tisdale
- **Leighton Meester**
- Lindsay Lohan
- Zooey Deschanel
Music and the Movies– 40 points

Kristen Stewart recently starred as which famous rock and roller in the film "Runaways"?
- **Joan Jett**
- Liz Phair
- Suzi Quatro
- Pat Benetar
Music and the Movies– 50 points

"Airplanes" by B.o.B. features which female singer from the band Paramore?
- Katy
- Alyssa
- **Hayley**
- Mary
Artists– 10 points

Who was the drummer in the band "The Beatles"?
- John Lennon
- Paul McCartney
- George Harrison
- **Ringo Starr**
Artists– 20 points

The Pop Group "Destiny's Child" was the original music group of what popular female artist?
- **Beyonce**
- Kesha
- Ciara
- Alicia Keys
Artists– 30 points

The band "The Script" is from which country?
- England
- Australia
- **Ireland**
- United States
Artists– 40 points

Lady Gaga's real name is:
- Angelica
- **Stefani**
- Amy
- Esmeralda

Artists– 50 points

7. Gather prizes. Library promotional items make great swag!

Room Set-up

Game console, instruments, microphone, projector, and screen at the front of the room

Chairs for drummer and guitarists

Tables and chairs at the back of the room for tweens who are waiting to perform

Program Outline

1. Formation of Teams: Divide tweens into teams. The number of people per team will depend on the number of instruments available. In our game system, there are four instruments, so four people per team. Some tweens will come to the program with a full team, while others will need additional players.

2. Band Names: Ask each team to come up with a band name, and even individual performer names if they wish.

3. The Tournament Begins: To determine which band plays first, draw names out of a hat or container. Ask the band which song they would like to perform. At the end of the song, record the score achieved by the band. Select the next band to play and repeat. The way in which your tournament brackets are set-up will determine the order of play. Play until a champion is crowned.

4. Music Jeopardy: Sometimes tweens are content to watch other bands while they play so they can size up the competition! Other times they may become bored and are looking for something to do while waiting for their turns. One option is to have an assortment of board and card games available. Another option is to have a laptop and a Microsoft® PowerPoint Jeopardy game running at the back of the room. Or, have a variety of worksheets, like the Jungle Word Scramble, available for tweens to complete.

5. Award prizes.

6. Clean up.

Materials Used

- Band Hero® or Rock Band® video game
- Video game console, projector, screen, video game instruments
- Laptop, and Microsoft® PowerPoint presentation
- Paper, pencil, and container
- Prizes

Budget

$0-$40 depending on the prizes offered

General Comments

Video gaming at the library can be a bit intimidating if you are not familiar with the various consoles and games. Find a staff member, student, or family member who can give you a tutorial to better understand what is involved. Gaming can be a costly endeavor with several initial expenses, but once the systems and games are purchased, there is virtually no cost to running these programs. If your library circulates video games, you won't even need to purchase a copy exclusively for program use. If you do decide to purchase a gaming system, ensure security measures are in place to prevent the theft of materials. Store in a locked cupboard and never leave unattended during a program. If you have a library system with multiple branches and are going to share consoles and games, create a system so that programs, consoles, and games are not double-booked. Not only is a gaming program easy to run with little preparation time required, but tweens will see the library as cool and cutting-edge, and appealing to their likes and interests. Since most tweens are playing video games anyway, they can play at the library where they can socialize with other tweens and enjoy the camaraderie of gaming on the big screen.

PREPARING FOR A JUNGLE BOOGIE SHOWDOWN WITH THE NINTENDO WII. COURTESY OF OSHAWA PUBLIC LIBRARIES GRAPHICS DEPARTMENT

TWIG: Tween Interest Group

Many libraries offer teen advisory boards, but few have organized advisory boards designed specifically for tweens. Since they want to be like their older teen counterparts, it only makes sense that tweens also want to have a sense of belonging and to make a difference at their library. Advisory boards or interest groups are a great way to develop deeper connections with your tween customers and to better understand what they want out of the library. Since meetings tend to be more laid back and informal, they often require less preparation time for library staff, which is always a bonus! While interest groups can be rolled out at any time of the year, it might be more advantageous to offer your first meeting over the summer months when tweens are actively looking for something to do. You might also wish to advertise this program to the schools in June in the hopes that friends might join together.

Program Advertisement

Have your say in library programs for your age group; review books, movies, music and video games; and participate in activities and games. Snacks provided.

Number of Spaces Available

20

Program Preparation (1-2 hours per month depending on activities offered)

1. When deciding to offer a tween interest group (TWIG), it is important to determine a meeting schedule. This includes frequency, as well as days and times. For continuity sake, one meeting per month is ideal; however, you may opt to offer more or less, depending on room availability and tween interest levels.

2. Decide if the program will be offered on a drop-in basis, or if registration will be required; there are merits to both options. Drop-in allows for a more casual atmosphere, but could leave you unsure of numbers for crafts, snacks, and activities. The best option may be to have tweens register initially but then drop-in for subsequent meetings.

3. Determine library tasks that would be appropriate for TWIG members to participate in. If you are working in a unionized environment and tweens are helping to run programs or assisting with shelf reading, be sure that union lines are not crossed.

4. Decide the other elements that will make up each TWIG meeting. Since there are no themes to TWIG meetings, the possibilities are endless. In fact, you could choose one or two elements from any program outline offered in this book. This is a great opportunity to "test drive" any program ideas you may have to see how feasible they really are. For a variety of ideas, see the Program Outline section below.

TWIG
Tween Interest Group

A new Tween Interest Group has launched at the Legends Centre Branch. Have your say in library programmes for your age group; review books, movies, music and video games; and participate in activities and games. Snacks will be provided.
<u>For ages 9-12.</u>

This is an ongoing programme that will meet on the first Thursday of every month at 7:00PM

- -

Name: _____   Date: _____

Address: _____

City: _____   Postal Code: _____

Phone: _____   School: _____   Grade: ____

Birth date: _____   Age: _____

Email Address: _____

Name of Parent(s)/Guardian(s): _____

OSHAWA
Public Libraries
far more than you expect

McLaughlin Branch	Jess Hann Branch	Northview Branch	Legends Centre Branch
65 Bagot Street	199 Wentworth St. W.	250 Beatrice St. E.	1661 Harmony Rd. N.
L1H 1N2	L1J 6P4	L1G 7T6	L1H 7K5

www.oshawalibrary.on.ca   905-579-6111

Room Set-up

Tables and chairs for crafts and activities

Bean bag chairs for discussions, circle games, or video games

Program Outline

1. Icebreaker: Choose any icebreaker from Chapter 3. Try a different one at each meeting.

2. Library Orientation: Before tweens can give their honest opinion about the collections, services, and programs they would like to see offered at the library, they must first have a good understanding of the library. Take tweens on a tour, highlighting collections, programs, and services for all ages. Encourage tweens to visit the library website and catalog. Scavenger hunts are a great way to make this more fun and less formal.

3. Feedback: Once tweens have an idea of all the library has to offer, ask for feedback and suggestions. Find out what *is* working well and any gaps that need to be filled. As a group, visit other library websites to determine what your organization might be lacking. Provide a list of possible ideas to gauge their interest level. Find out not only what will bring tweens and their peers to the library, but also what will keep them there. If tweens are hesitant to voice their opinions, hold a private vote or create a web survey that they can complete at home.

4. Library Helpers: One of the reasons tweens might enrol in TWIG is so that they can become involved in the daily operations of the library. Tweens are often extremely eager to help run activities and programs designed for pre-schoolers. Don't be surprised if they shy away from anything involving their peers, teens, or adults. Tweens are usually more comfortable working with younger children. The holidays are a good time to involve TWIG members in a preschool story time. Since many libraries offer special programs for Valentine's Day, Easter, Halloween, and Christmas, it is easy to make these TWIG-hosted events. During the program, enlist the help of TWIG members to hold the picture books, put the appropriate pieces on the felt board, hold a clothesline story, and lead the actions for participatory songs.

5. Book, DVD, and CD Reviews: Online customer reviews and ratings are a popular trend right now and are quickly becoming a standard in customer expectations. Websites like Amazon (*http://www.amazon.com*) and Chapters (*http://www.chapters.indigo.ca/home/*) are examples from the retail world, and the library world has followed suit by integrating social discovery software and enhanced content into online catalogs and websites. Numerous libraries are linking to review sites like Goodreads (*http://www.goodreads.com*), Shelfari (*http://www.shelfari.com*), and LibraryThing (*http://www.librarything.com*), or are moving toward ILS providers that integrate unique social software. To ensure that tween materials are being reviewed, ask TWIG members to write a review of the books that they read, DVDs that they watch, or CDs that they listen to. Tweens can be taught how to input the content themselves, or a hard copy can be brought to the library for staff to input at a later time. If your library receives advanced reading copies (ARCs), distribute them at TWIG meetings and ask for reviews to come back with the book. Tweens feel privileged to read a book before anyone else and think it is totally cool!

TWIG Review!

Attach another sheet or use back if necessary.

TITLE: _____

AUTHOR: _____

RATING: (Circle Total Number of Stars)

☆ ☆ ☆ ☆ ☆

REVIEW: _____

_____

_____

_____

_____

_____

_____

_____

_____

_____

_____

_____

YOUR INFO:

NAME: _____

6. Crafts: Depending on the interests of TWIG members, you may wish to offer crafts. Take a vote to find out if your tweens want to do crafts. Boys are not always interested.

7. Games: Have an assortment of board games and video games handy in case tweens want to play.

Materials Used

- This will depend upon the elements chosen for each meeting
- Snacks are a must!

Budget

$0-$50 per meeting. The bulk of your expense will usually be snacks.

General Comments

If your TWIG group is slow to start, be patient. Advertise in schools, change the day/time, or even move it to another library branch if needed. Once it is fully running, you and the tweens will have a blast!

Moon Day Party

July 20th marks the anniversary of our first contact with the moon! Kids of all ages love learning about space travel, so watch a few YouTube videos that talk about the moon landing; and if you have the Public Performance Rights, show snippets of a documentary on moon conspiracy theories, or a related Myth-Busters episode. This is a very versatile program that can fit many different themes, including fantasy, adventure, education, travel, and more!

Program Advertisement

43 years ago today, humans visited another world – the moon! Celebrate by making astronaut ice cream, eating moon pies, and exploring space conspiracies, like: did we ever really land on the moon?

Number of Spaces Available

20

Program Preparation (1-2 hours)

1. Gather supplies for moon pies and astronaut ice cream: for moon pies you can have them create their own by setting out cookies and icing (all different flavors and styles!) See below for astronaut ice cream.

2. Set up DVD player or laptop

3. If you would like to offer a craft, gather supplies such as clean rocks, glitter, glue, googly eyes—anything you feel would be appropriate for the tweens to decorate their moon rocks! You can even use glow-in the dark paint if you'd like.

Directions for Astronaut Ice Cream:

Astronaut ice cream, or freeze-dried ice cream, is the ultimate space food. It is simply ice cream that has had the water removed from it, and therefore requires no refrigeration. There are several ways to make Astronaut Ice Cream. If you have access to freeze drier or dehydrator, it is quite simple. First, freeze the ice cream covered in plastic wrap and make sure it is solid. Then wrap it in foil and follow the directions to your dehydrator. If you are a chemistry lover, you can turn this into a science experiment by making dry ice cream. You'll need:

- dry ice
- 2 cups heavy cream
- 2 cups half-and-half
- 3/4 cup sugar
- 2 teaspoons vanilla extract
- 1/8 teaspoon salt

4. Crush the dry ice. You can either place your dry ice in a paper bag and crush it with a large object like a mallet or hammer or roll over the bag using a rolling pin. Wear gloves while handling dry ice!

5. Mix all other ingredients in a large bowl. If you want a different flavor ice cream other than vanilla, add 1 cup of chocolate syrup for chocolate, 1 cup of strawberry syrup for strawberry, etc.

6, Shake/pour the dry ice into the ice cream, a tiny bit at a time, carefully mixing between additions. Continue to wear gloves as dry ice is EXTREMELY cold. You can get frostbite and not even realize it.

7. As you continue to add dry ice, it will begin to stiffen and will get increasingly difficult to mix. Continue to shake in dry ice until the ice cream has reached the consistency that you prefer.

8. Stir in any candy pieces, marshmallows, other flavors, etc.

9. The ice cream will be *very* cold! Do not eat right away because you can get frostbite..The ice cream is ready to safely eat when it is soft enough to scoop or stir.

10. You can freeze leftover ice cream to eat later.

Dry Ice Safety facts: *http://www.dryiceinfo.com/safe.htm*

Yet another way to make Astronaut Ice Cream is with a 'Dippin Dots Frozen Dot Maker' available online at: *http://www.amazon.com/Dippin-Dots-Frozen-Dot-Maker/dp/B002LDKKIQ*

Room Set-up

Tables and chairs for crafts and activities
Laptop or DVD player and projector

Program Outline

1. Icebreaker: Choose any icebreaker from Chapter 3. I had tweens tell me what they know about outer space and I learned quite a bit from them. For example, did you know the arm on space shuttles was made in Canada and is the known as the Canadarm?

2. Show time: Present conspiracy theories on the lunar landing. A great one is 2001's "Conspiracy Theory: Did We Land on the Moon?" There are many great videos on YouTube:

   http://youtu.be/Y5MVVtFYTSo

   http://youtu.be/t4tk-3KeYNQ

   http://youtu.be/Wym04J_3Ls0

   http://youtu.be/hMBCfuKs9i8

   This is a great way for tweens to practice their critical thinking skills. If the moon has no wind, then how was the flag moving on the flag pole? It's great for a healthy debate!

3. Have the tweens make their own moon pies (by making cookie sandwiches with frosting) and if you're brave, attempt 'Astronaut Ice Cream'

4. If you have time for a craft, tweens can have the tween create moon rocks or another outer space themed craft. There are many ideas online, especially at:

   http://www.4kraftykidz.com/OuterSpaceCrafts.html

Materials Used

- Moon landing conspiracy videos
- Laptop
- Projector
- Knives
- Freeze Drier/Dehydrator
- Astronaut Ice Cream supplies
- Ice Cream

Budget

$0-$50. The bulk of your expense will be snacks.

General Comments

If your library isn't open on July 20th, this program can be planned for anytime in July. Or you can switch up the month and just have a Blast Off! Party or another spacey theme.

Chapter 11: August

Congratulations on making it through a busy July! The first half of the summer may be over, but there is still much excitement to be had before the back-to-school routines begin. August can sometimes be a tricky month for programming; tweens either continue to swarm the library in droves, or they begin to tire of busy routines, opting for a break instead. Generally, programs offered at the beginning of the month may attract a larger audience than those offered during the last weeks of "freedom" for your tween library users. It is still imperative to offer programs to keep the momentum going and to build excitement for September's offerings. August's programs focus on reading club themes that have been stretched to include a building challenge, the ancient world, Steampunk and music.

Concrete Jungle

If you and your budget are feeling tired after a busy start to the summer, then this is the program for you. With minimal preparation and practically no cost, Concrete Jungle is a terrific choice for the end of August when attendance can be less predictable. There's nothing worse than planning an elaborate program and having no one show up. Regardless of when you offer this program, it is a fun building-themed competition that challenges tweens to put their imaginations and construction skills to the test.

Program Advertisement

Put your architectural skills to the test to create an urban masterpiece. A variety of building supplies will be provided and it will be up to you to out-build and out-last the competition.

Number of Spaces Available

20

Program Preparation (30 minutes)

1. Print out judging sheets.

2. Collect a variety of supplies that can be used as building materials.

3. Pull any books in your collection that contain pictures of famous structures. Suggestions include the Statue of Liberty, Golden Gate Bridge, CN Tower, Eiffel Tower, Leaning Tower of Pisa, Taj Mahal, Petronas Towers, Machu Picchu, etc.

Room Set-up

5 tables with 4 chairs around each

2 tables for building supplies

Program Outline

1. Icebreaker: Ask tweens to state their names and any building experience that they have, for example, anything they may have built with a parent, at school, or in the backyard. As a group, create a list of famous structures.

2. Formation of Teams: Divide tweens into groups of no more than four.

3. Explain the Rules:

   - Each team will be responsible for creating two structures: one imitation structure and one free-style structure.

   - The imitation structure will be judged based on structural integrity, creativity, visual effect, and likeness to the real structure. There must be a photo of the chosen structure in the available books so that the judges can compare its likeness.

   - The free-style structure will be judged based on use of materials, structural integrity, creativity, and visual effect.

   - Teams may use only the materials provided, and each team member must contribute.

   - Each structure must be given a name.

   - When the allotted time is up, each tween will choose their favorite imitation and free-style structure and record their votes on the judging sheets. Tweens cannot vote for their own team's creation.

4. Build-off: Clearly state that each team will have approximately 20 minutes to build each structure and let the fun begin! If you find that projects are taking longer than anticipated, offer a time extension.

5. Tally Votes: Once the votes are tallied, announce the winner in each category.

6. Award Prizes.

7. Clean up.

Free-Style Architecture

Please judge on use of materials, structural integrity, creativity and visual effect.

My favourite structure is:

_____

** You cannot vote for your own structure **

Free-Style Architecture

Please judge on use of materials, structural integrity, creativity and visual effect.

My favourite structure is:

_____

** You cannot vote for your own structure **

Free-Style Architecture

Please judge on use of materials, structural integrity, creativity and visual effect.

My favourite structure is:

_____

** You cannot vote for your own structure **

Free-Style Architecture

Please judge on use of materials, structural integrity, creativity and visual effect.

My favourite structure is:

_____

** You cannot vote for your own structure **

Free-Style Architecture

Please judge on use of materials, structural integrity, creativity and visual effect.

My favourite structure is:

_____

** You cannot vote for your own structure **

Free-Style Architecture

Please judge on use of materials, structural integrity, creativity and visual effect.

My favourite structure is:

_____

** You cannot vote for your own structure **

Imitation Architecture	Imitation Architecture
Please judge on structural integrity, creativity, visual effect and likeness to the real structure.	Please judge on structural integrity, creativity, visual effect and likeness to the real structure.
My favourite structure is:	My favourite structure is:
_____	_____
** You cannot vote for your own structure **	** You cannot vote for your own structure **
Imitation Architecture	Imitation Architecture
Please judge on structural integrity, creativity, visual effect and likeness to the real structure.	Please judge on structural integrity, creativity, visual effect and likeness to the real structure.
My favourite structure is:	My favourite structure is:
_____	_____
** You cannot vote for your own structure **	** You cannot vote for your own structure **
Imitation Architecture	Imitation Architecture
Please judge on structural integrity, creativity, visual effect and likeness to the real structure.	Please judge on structural integrity, creativity, visual effect and likeness to the real structure.
My favourite structure is:	My favourite structure is:
_____	_____
** You cannot vote for your own structure **	** You cannot vote for your own structure **

Materials Used

- Paper and pencils for judging sheets
- Books containing pictures of famous structures
- Building supplies
    - Construction paper and/or Bristol board
    - Toothpicks
    - Tape
    - Glue
    - Sticky Tack
    - Paper towel rolls
    - String
    - Cardboard
    - Disposable cups
    - Pom poms
    - Gimp
    - Styrofoam balls
    - Newspaper
    - Pipe cleaners
    - Aluminum foil
    - Building blocks
    - Tongue depressors
    - Scissors
    - Markers
    - Marshmallows
- CD player and CD so that music can be played while the tweens are working

Budget

$0-$50. Most of the materials used in this program can be found in the library or collected from home and coworkers.

General Comments

Depending on how meticulous the tweens are when creating their structures, you may not have time for both imitation and free-style building. If you do run out of time, consider offering this program a second time with either the same or different building supplies.

Relic Hunter

With the abundance of innovative and high-tech gadgets available today, it is surprising how many tweens enjoy delving into the past to discover ancient artifacts and relics. This scavenger hunt-based program is an excellent opportunity for tweens to explore the library and the past, while participating in an exciting adventure. This is also a great way to attract tween boys to the library, especially those who are fans of Indiana Jones!

Program Advertisement

Do you like adventure and archaeology? Do you want to be the next Indiana Jones? Join us as we hunt for clues to find the lost, stolen, or hidden treasures!

Number of Spaces Available

20

Program Preparation (1 hour)

1. Several days before the program, create the fossils: Mix 4 cups flour, 1 ½ cups salt, and 1 ½ cups water. This will make several fossils. Multiply the recipe as needed. Form each fossil into the shape of your choice, and insert a small trinket into the center. Trinket ideas include a bead or a small toy figurine. The fossils will take approximately 2 days to harden; do *not* bake them in the oven. The recipe is also available online at *http://www.kidsrcrafty.com/self-hardening_clay.htm.*

2. Print the ancient Egyptian hieroglyphics hand-out.

3. Print the ancient scrolls and hide them behind books in the 932 (Dewey Decimal) section.

4. Print the labyrinth maze.

5. Use the following list as a starting point to find and print images for the Describe the Relic game. Be sure to print a corresponding list of details as well, so that you can give tweens the correct answer.

> Inca wooden drinking vessel, Peru, late 17th - 18th century: *http://www.britishmuseum.org/explore/highlights/highlight_objects/aoa/i/inca_wooden_drinking_vessel.aspx*
>
> Moche warrior pot, Peru, A.D. 100-700: *http://www.britishmuseum.org/explore/highlights/highlight_objects/aoa/m/moche_warrior_pot.aspx*
>
> Terracotta army, China, 221 BC: *http://whc.unesco.org/en/list/441*
>
> Runestone, Denmark, A.D. 965: *http://www.pbs.org/wgbh/nova/ancient/viking-runes-through-time.html*
>
> Battersea cauldron, England, 800-700 BC: *http://www.britishmuseum.org/explore/highlights/highlight_objects/pe_prb/t/the_battersea_cauldron.aspx*

HIEROGLYPHICS

Solve the Code for a Hidden Message!

___ __ ___   ___ __ __ __ __ __

___ __ __ __   __ __ __ __

___ __ __ __   ___ __   __ __ __ __ __ __

__ __ __   ___ __ ___

___ __ __ __
___

HIEROGLYPHICS

A	B	C	D	E	F		J	H

G	K	L	M	N	O	W	U

R	S	T	TH	YI		Z	KH-CH

	1
	10
	100
	1000
	10,000
	100,000
	1,000,000

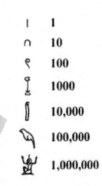

o the _____ you must go,

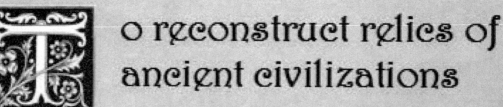o reconstruct relics of ancient civilizations

Oh No!

You're lost in an ancient Greek labyrinth! Starting from the center, see if you can find your way out alive...

You Made It!

Maze From: KRAZYDAD.COM/PUZZLES

Wine vessel, China, 13th-12th century BC: *http://www.britishmuseum.org/explore/highlights/highlight_objects/asia/b/bronze_zun_ritual_wine_vessel.aspx*

Arrow point, Canada, A.D. 1100-1700: *http://www.nmai.si.edu/searchcollections/item.aspx?irn=163537&catids=2&objtypeid=Hunting/Fishing/Warfare\Arrow%20point&src=1-4*

Mayan vase, Guatemala, A.D. 600-800: *http://www.britishmuseum.org/explore/highlights/highlight_objects/aoa/t/the_fenton_vase.aspx*

Ming banknote, China, A.D. 1375: *http://www.britishmuseum.org/explore/highlights/highlight_objects/cm/c/chinese_ming_bank_note.aspx*

Mask, Japan, 18th-19th century A.D.: *http://www.britishmuseum.org/explore/highlights/highlight_objects/asia/n/n%C5%8D_mask_known_as_hannya.aspx*

Pendant, Egypt, 11th century A.D.: *http://www.britishmuseum.org/explore/highlights/highlight_objects/me/g/gold_pendant_with_enamel.aspx*

Room Set-up

5 tables for pyramid building and fossil picking, with 4 chairs each

Program Outline

1. Icebreaker: Ask tweens to arrange themselves in order of their birthdays, but do not allow them to say the day or month.

2. Formation of Teams: Divide tweens into groups of two. If there are uneven numbers, you can have a team of three.

3. Ancient Egyptian Hieroglyphics: Give each team the ancient Egyptian hieroglyphics hand-out to decipher. This will be their first clue in the competition and will lead them to the scrolls that are hidden in the 932 section of the library.

4. Ancient Scrolls: Once tweens find these scrolls, they will be directed to another location to complete their next task.

5. Sugar Cube Pyramid Building: Using sugar cubes, tweens will build a pyramid. Make sure that each team has the same number of cubes so that no one is at a disadvantage.

6. Labyrinth Maze: As teams finish their sugar cube pyramid, distribute the labyrinth maze handout to complete.

7. Toilet Paper Mummies: When all teams have completed the labyrinth maze, choose the two tallest tweens in the group. These two tweens will be wrapped in toilet paper. Divide the remaining tweens into two groups. One group will work together to wrap the first tween, while the other group will wrap the second. So that everyone gets a chance to wrap, you can limit the time each tween wraps.

8. Fossils: Reassign tweens to their original groups of two and give each team a fossil. Using toothpicks, tweens chip away at the fossils to reveal treasures.

9. Describe the Relic: Bring all tweens together as one big group to play this fun guessing game. Give each tween a picture of an ancient relic. They must then describe their relic to the group, including details such as country of origin, use, and time period from which it comes. Ask others for their input before revealing the correct answer.

10. Award Prizes: Even though tweens are divided into teams, much of this program is a group effort. As a result, there is not really a winning team. Ideally everyone would go home with a prize, but if this is not possible, consider awarding a prize to the best pyramid builders or the person who correctly identified an ancient relic.

11. Clean up.

Materials Used

- Toilet paper
- Pencils
- Salt
- Flour
- Water
- Trinkets for the fossils
- Sugar cubes

Budget

Approximately $15 for sugar cubes and flour

General Comments

The relic describing activity was extremely popular, with many tweens wanting multiple turns. You may want to print out a few extra for this purpose. As mentioned earlier, this program was very successful in attracting a lot of tween boys to the library, which can sometimes be difficult. If you have a lot of Indiana Jones fans, consider re-naming the program to reflect this. Just be careful that the overt title doesn't deter non-Indiana Jones fans!

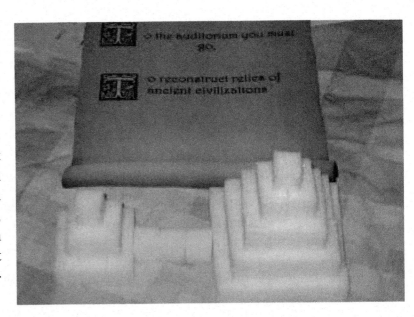

Tribal Beats

Unbeknownst to tweens, this program is actually based on the casserole, or 'Pots and Pans,' movement used as a form of protest in many Spanish speaking countries and, most recently, Montreal. It consists of a group of people banging together any household object they can find in order to bring attention to their cause. It's fun to make noise at any age! In this program, tweens are encouraged to create noisemakers and toot their own horns!

Program Advertisement

Have a musical talent? Share it with others at this exciting event as we make our own instruments and celebrate with our tribe!

Number of Spaces Available

20

Program Preparation (45 minutes)

1. Make some sample instruments. Create a shaker using a paper-towel tube and beans or rice or whatever else you'd like to fill it with. Cover the ends of the tube with paper, fabric, or aluminum foil. Another shaker can be made using two paper plates: Decorate the paper plates, add bells or beans in one, place the other on top and staple all around. Attach ribbon and voila--a homemade tambourine! Additional shaker designs are available online at *http://www.kidscraftweekly.com/music_issue.html.* Participants may create instruments other than shakers.

2. Collect a variety of supplies that can be glued onto the shakers or other instruments they chose to create. We printed out animal/safari prints to decorate the shakers, and supplied beads and glitter.

3. Print out any word searches or word scrambles on music. Why reinvent the wheel? Try one of these available online: *http://homeschooling.about.com/od/freeprintables/ss/musicprint_all.htm.*

4. Pull any books in your collection that explain how to make musical instruments.

Room Set-up

5 tables with 4 chairs around each

1 table for craft supplies

Program Outline

1. Icebreaker: Since this is a musical event, ask the tweens to share their names and whether or not they play a musical instrument. If they don't play one, which instrument would they love to learn how to play?

2. Explain how to make the shakers, showing the examples you made.

3. Play music: Tune the radio to the tweens favorite music station. While they create their instruments, ask what their favorite kinds of music and favorite songs are and other music related questions.

4. Word Searches, Word Scrambles: Have word searches and scrambles or other puzzles on hand for tweens to complete if they finish their craft early.

5. Tribal Beat Parade! This is optional, but oh-so-fun! The tweens lead a parade with their newly created musical instruments--either in the children's section of the library or down the sidewalk, depending on your library's location.

6. Clean up.

Materials Used

- Paper
- Books containing information about instruments
- Instrument Materials
    - Construction paper and/or Bristol board
    - Water bottles
    - Tape
    - Glue
    - Sticky Tack
    - Paper towel rolls
    - String
    - Paper plates
    - Cardboard
    - Pom poms
    - Styrofoam balls
    - Newspaper
    - Pipe cleaners
    - Aluminum foil
    - Scissors
    - Markers
    - Bells, beans, rice, or corn--something to put inside your music maker
- CD player and CD or radio so that music can be played while the tweens are working

Budget

$0-$10. Most of the materials used in this program can be collected and donated.

General Comments

We didn't know how this would go over because creating instruments is something that is often done at Pre-School Story Time. Fortunately, it went over super well! The participants loved creating a way to be loud in the library and we loved getting rid of old craft supplies. Win-win!

SAMPLING SOME TUNES AT THE LISTENING STATION. COURTESY OF OSHAWA PUBLIC LIBRARIES

Steampunk DIY Tea Party

Steampunk is really big right now in some circles. Either you know Steampunk or you don't. What is Steampunk? According to Steampunk.com, "Steampunk has always been first and foremost a literary genre, or least a subgenre of science fiction and fantasy that includes social or technological aspects of the 19th century (the steam) usually with some deconstruction of, reimagining of, or rebellion against parts of it (the punk)." You can get rid of the tea party if you'd like and just have a craft program.

Program Advertisement

Do you know what Steampunk is? Join us for an event that is part Gothic Victorian Tea Party, part do-it-yourself extravaganza. While you enjoy your tea and scones, learn how to create crafts with a Steampunk twist!

Number of Spaces Available

20

Program Preparation (2 hours)

1. Decide and prepare the crafts that you'd like to introduce.

2. If you're having a tea party, pick up the supplies for tea. We did hot and iced tea options.

3. If you want to decorate, research Steampunk and create centerpieces or visit a party store for ideas.

4. Contact your local Steampunk society for ideas or advertising.

Room Set-up

Tables and chairs for crafts

Program Outline

1. Icebreaker: Pick out a great icebreaker from Chapter 3. You can ask the tweens if they know what Steampunk is.

2. Show photos of Steampunk. If you're feeling really industrious, wear a Steampunk costume yourself!

3. Offer crafts. Here are several to try:

   Part 1 – Locket

   - Using a regular hinge, small piece of wire and ball chain, create locket by pasting pictures on inside of the hinge, and attaching wire to hinge, leaving small loop for chain to go through.

Part 2 – Goggles

- Alter two toilet paper rolls so they fit comfortably around the eyes. Cut out two circles the same size as the circumference of the toilet paper rolls. Cut out middle of circle. Using discarded TP roll pieces, cut two circles free and extend them a tiny bit by adding some thin cardboard to their circumference. Using masking tape, attach this roll piece to cardboard circle.

- Take plastic laminate and cut two circles the same size as the cardboard pieces. Stick together to create a lens. Glue lenses to cardboard pieces.

- Attach lens frames to eye pieces with tape. Attach eyepieces together with soft wire. Tape over soft wire on inside and outside if you'd like for the nose piece. Paint.

- Attach elastic cord with split pins to sides of eye pieces for a headband. Tape over split pins (on inside) to hold in place.

Part 3 – Keychain

- Take metal washer and secure brass fastener through hole in middle to look like watch arms. Take second fastener (with small loop of chain in between legs) and glue to back of washer. Take jump ring and glue to front (careful not to catch arms underneath). Attach to key ring.

4. While the tweens are working on their crafts, offer tea and scones. We ordered our scones through a wholesaler.

5. Clean up.

Materials Used

- Toilet paper rolls
- Iced tea
- Scones
- Hot tea
- Teapots
- Washers
- Gears
- Tissue paper
- Small hinges
- Split pins
- Thin cardboard
- Keychain rings
- Chain
- Wire
- Masking tape

- Duct tape
- (2 pictures)
- Paint
- Laminate
- Elastic cord

Budget

$20-$60. You can always ask for donations or visit the dollar store.

General Comments

You could call this program something else if you are not offering tea, like Get Steampunk'd! There are many variations available and the Internet and Pinterest have a million Steampunk ideas! I thought that the iced tea would be most popular with the tweens but I was wrong – everyone wanted hot tea! Maybe it's Canada's British roots. . . .

Chapter 12: September

"There comes a time when autumn asks, 'What have you been doing all summer?'" (Anon). Why, library programming, of course! You may be tempted to take a break after a busy summer, but try to keep the momentum going. If you continue providing programs for the tweens who spent the summer with you, they will gladly follow you through the rest of the year. Yet, the first two weeks of September can be difficult for library programming. Tweens and their parents are getting used to a new routine for school, one that doesn't yet include the library. They will be knocking on your door soon, looking for something fun to do. This September, celebrate school and Bilbo and Frodo's birthday with two terrific parties, play a wild game of musical chairs, and learn how to start a book club designed especially for tweens and their mothers.

Back to School Bash

While some tweens cringe at the thought of going back to school, others simply can't wait to get their new pencils and notebooks in order. The library is a terrific place to begin! This program is unique because it was hosted by the library's teen advisory board in conjunction with library staff. The older teens helped tweens decorate school supplies, and even came up with a few designs of their own. While this is a perfect program to offer in any community, it is especially ideal for high-risk or impoverished neighborhoods where students cannot always afford new supplies. Partner with local office supply stores to get discounts on the products you'll be giving away.

Program Advertisement

You have your binders and books, now it's time to decorate them! Come party with us and start the school year off right! Fun crafts, activities, and more! Win free school supplies! Hosted by the teen advisory board!

Number of Spaces Available

20

Program Preparation (1 hour)

1. Purchase an assortment of school supplies.

2. Purchase and stuff the piñata.

3. Gather and/or purchase craft and cookie decorating supplies.

4. Print the back to school word scramble and trivia.

5. Wrap a school supply item with multiple layers of paper for Pass the School Supply.

6. Gather novels that take place in a school for a school-themed book display.

Room Set-up

An open space for Pass the School Supply and School Supply Piñata

A table and chairs for the "Cookie Decorating Station"

A table and chairs for the "Craft Corner." One table per craft is recommended.

Program Outline

1. Icebreaker: Ask tweens and teen advisory board members to state their names, and what their favorite and least favorite school subjects are.

2. Pass the School Supply: Start the program with a tween version of the lively party game, Pass the Parcel. Choose a school supply to wrap in paper numerous times. Use a different color of paper for each layer and write a "task" on each layer. Task ideas include: tell a funny joke, do the chicken dance, repeat this tongue twister, sing a song, etc. Begin the game by playing music. As the music plays, tweens pass the wrapped school supply from one to the other in a circle. When the music stops, the tween holding the parcel must un-wrap one layer of paper and perform the task written on the layer below. Repeat until the parcel is fully un-wrapped. The last person to un-wrap the school supply is the winner and keeps the item.

3. School Supply Piñata: If you have a larger space or access to the outdoors, give tweens the chance to put on a blindfold and take a swing at a piñata filled with school supplies. Tweens can hit the pinata with a yardstick, baseball bat, or even use their bare hands. Ensure the other program participants stand well behind the tween swinging at the pinata so no one gets hurt. When the piñata breaks, make sure everyone gets an assortment of goods by allowing only one type of supply per tween (one eraser, one pencil, one notepad, etc.).

Back To School Word Scramble

Iepinc ___ ___ ___ ___ ___ ___

Oobsk ___ ___ ___ ___

Neps ___ ___ ___ ___

Galhncub ___ ___ ___ ___ ___ ___ ___

Soclhobsu ___ ___ ___ ___ ___ ___ ___ ___ ___

Ssecer ___ ___ ___ ___ ___ ___

Atmh ___ ___ ___ ___

Rsyioth ___ ___ ___ ___ ___ ___ ___

Oahgregyp ___ ___ ___ ___ ___ ___ ___ ___ ___

Reahctse ___ ___ ___ ___ ___ ___ ___ ___

Utdsent ___ ___ ___ ___ ___ ___ ___

Rsserae ___ ___ ___ ___ ___ ___ ___

Ekdss ___ ___ ___ ___ ___

Back to School Trivia

1.   What color are most school buses painted?

2.   What invention inspired the creation of glue sticks?
   a.   Popsicles
   b.   Lollipops
   c.   Lipstick

3.   How many words can a typical pencil write before it is unusable?
   a.   10,000 words
   b.   25,000 words
   c.   45,000 words

4.   I am usually yellow with a pink tip. What am I?

5.   What is the name of the teacher who takes her students on field trips in an unusual school bus?
   a.   Miss. Sizzle
   b.   Miss. Frizzle
   c.   Miss. Twizzle

6.   On which floor of Wayside School is the cafeteria located?
   a.   5
   b.   10
   c.   15

7.   What is a pencil made of?
   a.   Lead
   b.   Carbon
   c.   Silver

8.   When the teacher wants students to be quiet, yet entertained during indoor recess, what game is usually played?
   a.   Marco Polo
   b.   Red Rover, Red Rover
   c.   7-up

Answer Key:

Yellow; C- lipstick; C-4500; pencil; B- Miss. Frizzle; C-15; A-lead; C-7-up

4. Craft Corner: Give each tween a cloth pencil case to decorate using fabric paint, sequins, and glue. Binders, notebooks, pocket folders can be decorated using markers, foam craft shapes, sequins, ribbon, and glue. Cork boards for lockers can be made by gluing two magnets to the back of a piece of cork. The front can be decorated with glitter glue, foam craft shapes, ribbon, and glue.

5. Cookie Decorating Station: Provide an assortment of cookies that can be iced and decorated at a crafty snack station. Provide water or juice so tweens can wash the cookies down.

6. Back to School Worksheets: Provide an assortment of back to school trivia and word scramble worksheets for tweens who finish the other activities early.

7. Clean up. Ask teen advisory board members to help with the clean up. It will go much faster!

Materials Used

- School supply for Pass the School Supply
- Various colors of paper for wrapping
- Tape
- Pen
- CD player
- CD
- Piñata
- A rope or cord to suspend the piñata
- Yardstick or bat
- Blindfold
- An assortment of school supplies for the piñata (erasers, pencils, repositionable notes, notebooks, highlighters, glue sticks, etc.)
- Cloth pencil cases
- Binders, duo tangs, folders, notebooks
- Fabric paint
- Sequins
- Foam craft shapes
- Ribbon
- Glitter glue
- White glue
- Rolls of cork
- Magnets
- An assortment of cookies
- Icing/Frosting
- Sprinkles
- Candies

Budget

Approximately $100. Since school supplies can be expensive, ask for donations from your local office supply store. Dollar or discount stores also offer great deals. You may also wish to choose a craft that uses materials you already have on-hand.

General Comments

This program was such a hit that it was difficult to tell who had more fun: the tweens attending or the teens running the program! If teen advisory board members are running this program (with the help of library staff), expect teens to fully participate in all activities and crafts. This means buying extra quantities of everything. If you have 20 tweens attending and 20 teens attending, buy 40 of everything! Another helpful hint: don't wear your good clothes if you are using fabric paint to decorate the pencil cases. You may want to put a disclaimer in the advertisement so that tweens wear old clothes.

Happy Birthday to the Hobbits!

If you've read J. R. R. Tolkien's *Lord of the Rings*, you'll know that hobbits are a fictional race that inhabit the lands of Middle-Earth. Perhaps the most famous hobbits of all are Bilbo and Frodo Baggins, who both celebrate their birthday on September 22. What better way to celebrate this momentous day than with a birthday party of epic proportions!

Program Advertisement

Celebrate Bilbo and Frodo's birthday at the library! Come prepared for *Lord of the Rings* trivia, crafts, food, and more! The best dressed hobbit will win a prize!

Number of Spaces Available

20

Program Preparation (1 hour)

1. Pull any *Lord of the Rings* related books and read-alikes for a display.

2. Purchase or print life-size pictures of hobbits.

3. Print the hobbit word search. Search the Internet for the Elvish alphabet and print.

4. Determine which items will be used for the scavenger hunt and print any necessary images. Place these items and images throughout the room. Print a list of hidden items for each tween.

5. Pre-order a birthday cake. Purchase drinks and prizes.

Hobbit Word Search

r	s	s	p	n	o	n	e	p	d	n	n	a	m	i	l	g	i	m	r
e	m	i	h	e	s	w	u	s	b	g	m	s	o	e	g	n	d	e	r
s	a	s	t	i	n	g	i	m	i	u	i	g	p	g	p	d	r	u	f
s	u	p	a	r	r	a	r	i	l	l	o	y	a	o	o	b	m	f	n
r	g	r	e	l	r	e	d	l	b	g	r	a	t	r	r	m	l	p	n
g	t	a	s	l	s	b	o	d	o	r	f	p	a	t	a	n	m	u	r
a	e	g	n	i	r	g	e	r	e	p	n	o	g	g	s	o	e	i	r
s	r	r	w	d	g	o	c	m	i	o	m	e	p	s	o	g	o	f	o
m	o	m	p	r	a	b	n	p	i	b	y	h	s	a	g	g	e	i	e
n	a	e	n	r	i	l	p	d	e	c	o	c	y	g	d	l	f	i	s
s	i	n	p	l	b	i	f	t	d	d	t	r	i	r	e	r	o	l	d
i	l	g	h	l	n	n	g	s	b	g	d	r	r	l	r	l	l	n	n
r	s	r	g	r	g	s	m	e	w	s	o	g	r	d	e	a	o	o	m
s	d	s	e	b	e	n	t	u	r	s	i	i	g	t	e	i	l	s	a
m	r	p	e	e	l	a	s	n	i	n	p	o	a	e	g	n	m	r	b
e	l	f	a	l	o	g	g	s	g	m	l	p	i	o	m	p	d	s	e
b	d	r	s	u	r	l	g	r	t	r	a	e	a	l	i	r	o	r	i
i	g	n	u	a	p	e	r	e	r	g	n	l	l	e	n	y	p	r	i
e	d	o	y	b	h	m	p	o	s	e	n	g	n	i	i	i	g	i	n
i	i	r	l	b	a	n	a	g	o	o	r	r	r	p	n	r	g	i	r

Gollum	**Pippin**	**Samwise**
Sting	**Shire**	**Peregrin**
Orc	**Ring**	**Gandalf**
Goblins	**Elrond**	**Frodo**
Merry	**Smaug**	**Bilbo**

Room Set-up

A table and chairs for each Hobbit Jeopardy team
Screen, projector, and laptop/computer
An open space for circle games

Program Outline

1. Take Your Picture with a Hobbit: Here is a great opportunity for tweens to have their photo taken with a hobbit! If you have the resources available, provide a life-size cut-out of hobbits so that tweens can take their picture with the birthday boys! Tweens can either use their own cameras or you can take their picture and email it to them at a later date or post it on the library website/Facebook page if photo release forms have been signed. Cardboard cut-outs can either be purchased online at *http://www.lotrfanshop.com/lotrshop/standups.asp*, or can be printed on a large-scale printer. A sample photo release form can be found on page 179.

2. Write Your Name in Elvish: Using the Elvish alphabet you found online, tweens make nametags with their Elvish names.

3. Biggest Birthday Greeting Game: This game requires tweens to sit in a circle and use their imagination to tell a story. The first party guest tells the Birthday Hobbit, "I was coming to give you your birthday greeting when _____," and proceeds to account some outrageous event that occurred on the way to the party. The second guest says "Well, that was rare indeed, but when I was coming to give you your birthday greeting _____," and tries to top the first guest's story. The game is over when a guest cannot think of a story to top the last one. Additional information about this game is available online at *http://www.hobbithappybirthday.com/hobbit_birthday_party_games.shtml*.

4. Not-So Secret Scavenger Hunt: Most scavenger hunts involve searching for hidden clues, but this one requires tweens to search an open space for some not so well-hidden objects. Take some of the objects listed above (some of them are permanent fixtures and may already be in the room) and "hide" them in plain sight, but in an unexpected place. Instead of the actual object, you may wish to print an image of an item. Give each tween a list of these objects and ask them to check off each item they find. They must not move the item and must be as discreet as possible when they find it so they don't tip off their fellow competitors. The first tween to find all of the items gets to choose the first prize, and so-on until all tweens have finished and received a prize.

Scavenger Hunt Items
- Paper clip
- Violets
- Red tissue paper
- Electrical outlet
- Pen
- Tablecloth
- Hinge
- Fire alarm bell
- Pumpkin
- The letter "C"
- A picture of Dora
- Staple
- Wheel
- Suction cup
- Door knob
- Backspace key
- A shark
- Door stopper
- Butterfly
- A puppet
- A magazine
- Exit sign
- A leaf

Photographs and Video Consent, Waiver, Indemnity and Release

Photographs, Videos and Recordings

I hereby grant permission to Oshawa Public Libraries to take photographs or videos of me and to make recordings of my voice at the event or location noted below.

First and Last Name:	
Organization:	
Email:	
Phone:	
Parent/Guardian (if under age 18):	
Event/Location:	
Date:	

I further grant to Oshawa Public Libraries the right to reproduce, use, exhibit, display, broadcast and distribute and create derivative works of these images and recordings in any media now known or later developed as well as my name for promoting and/or publicizing Oshawa Public Libraries. I acknowledge that Oshawa Public Libraries owns all rights to the images and recordings.

Waiver, Indemnity and Release

I hereby waive any right to inspect or approve the use of the images or recordings or of any written copy.

I am 18 years of age or older and I am competent to contract in my own name. I have read this document before signing below, and I fully understand the contents, meaning and impact of this consent, waiver, indemnity and release.

_____   _____
Signature (if age 18 or older)   Date

_____   _____
Signature of Parent/Guardian (if under age 18)   Date

_____   _____
Signature of Witness   Date

Personal information is collected under the authority of the Public Libraries Act, R.S.O. 1990, for the purposes of providing Library service responsive to our community's unique needs. Questions about the collection of personal information should be directed to the CEO, Oshawa Public Libraries, 65 Bagot Street, Oshawa, ON L1H 1N2 (905) 579-6111 ext. 5212.

5. Hobbit Jeopardy: Finally the moment everyone has been waiting for—a chance to show-off their hobbit trivia knowledge! Divide tweens into 3 or 4 teams, trying to evenly distribute those with little knowledge of *Lord of the Rings* and hobbits amongst those who do (tweens may attend a program even if they have little knowledge of the theme). Allow each team to choose a team name and a captain. As the questions are revealed, each captain will record the team's answer on a whiteboard or piece of paper. Each captain will simultaneously reveal his or her team's answer. Award the correct number of points to each team that has the correct answer. Continue until all questions have been revealed and a winner has been crowned. A Microsoft® PowerPoint version of Hobbit Jeopardy is also available online at *https://sites.google.com/site/thetweenscene/*.

Questions for Hobbit Jeopardy

Hobbits – 10 points: Hobbits have very hairy…

    Faces   *Feet*   Chests   Heads

Hobbits – 20 points: How tall are hobbits?

    Two Feet Tall   *Between Two and Four Feet*   Four to Five Feet Tall   One to Two Feet Tall

Hobbits – 30 points: How Long is the Hobbit Life Expectancy?

    50 Years   80 Years   *100 Years*   They can live forever unless killed

Hobbits – 40 points: How many "breeds" of hobbits are there?

    Just One   Two   *Three*   Too Many to Count

Hobbits – 50 points: How many meals a day do hobbits eat?

    Just one   Two   Five   *At least seven*

Home and Culture – 10 points: In what sort of buildings do Hobbits live?

    Holes in hills or the ground   Small wooden buildings

    Outside, under the trees   in large farmhouses with their whole families

Home and Culture– 20 points: What tradition do Shire hobbits have on their birthdays?

    They invite everyone in the town   *They give gifts instead of receiving them*

    The festivities last for one week   They don't have to do any work

Home and Culture– 30 points: When does a hobbit come of age?

    18   25   *33*   72

Home and Culture– 40 points: Hobbits are descendants of which race?

    Humans   Dwarfs   Elves   Trolls

Home and Culture– 50 points: The Shire, where Bilbo and Frodo live, is on the side of what river?

    Shire River   The Misty River   Bree River   *Brandywine*

Bilbo's Adventures– 10 points: Who visits Bilbo right at the start of "The Hobbit"?

    A dwarf   An angry troll   His neighbour   *Gandalf the wizard*

Bilbo's Adventures– 20 points: How many dwarves did Bilbo set out with on his adventure?

    2   10   *13*   Two Dozen

Bilbo's Adventures– 30 points: What was special about the sword Bilbo got from the Trolls?

    It never failed to kill   *It turned blue when orcs were nearby*

    It shrinks to the right size of whoever holds it   It could turn people to stone

Bilbo's Adventures– 40 points: What was in Bilbo's pocket when Gollum tried to guess?

    A ring   Nothing   Hands   String

Bilbo's Adventures– 50 points: Bilbo's quest was to steal back the treasure of the dwarves from…

    The Goblins   Sauron the Wizard   The Orcs   *Smaug the Dragon*

Frodo's Adventures– 10 points: Where is Frodo's ultimate destination?

    Mount Doom   The Edge of the Earth   Dead Marshes   Gondor

Frodo's Adventures– 20 points: Frodo is Bilbo's…

    Nephew   *Cousin*   Son   They are not actually related

Frodo's Adventures– 30 points: At the end of the *Lord of the Rings*, Bilbo, Gandalf, Frodo and the Elves set off for…

    The End of the World   The Land Across the Sea   *The Undying Lands*   Lower Earth

Frodo's Adventures– 40 points: Including Frodo's ring, how many rings of power were made?

    5   10   15   *20*

Frodo's Adventures– 50 points: Who attacks Frodo when he is about to throw the ring into Mount Doom?

    Gollum   Gandalf   Bilbo   Saruman

Hobbit Friends– 10 points: How many hobbit companions does Frodo arrive in Rivendell with?

    1   2   3   *4*

Hobbit Friends– 20 points: After Gandalf dies, he returns as Gandalf the…

    Grey   Silver   *White*   Great

Hobbit Friends– 30 points: Samwise Gamgee, Frodo's trusted friend, was originally his…

    Neighbor   Cousin   Sheppard   *Gardner*

Hobbit Friends– 40 points: Who do Frodo and his friends meet at the Inn of the Prancing Pony?

    Aragorn   Arwin   Elrond   Gandalf

Hobbit Friends– 50 points: Which elven friend of the Hobbits refuses the ring, because it would make them "beautiful and terrible"?

    Elrond   Arwin   *Galadriel*   Gildor

6.   Hobbit Feet craft: To make hobbit feet, glue pieces of brown yarn onto the top of a pair of socks.

7.   Birthday Cake: Serve a cake that says "Happy Birthday, Hobbits!" Serve water or juice boxes.

8.   Award for Best Costume: If, in your advertisement, you encouraged tweens to come dressed as a hobbit, award a prize for the best costume. You may wish to have tweens vote for their favorite or you may wish to give everyone a prize.

9.   Clean up.

Materials Used

- Hobbit cardboard cut-out
- Camera (optional)
- Tape
- Nametags
- Markers
- Scavenger hunt items
- Pencils
- Whiteboards
- Dry Erase markers
- Laptop/Computer
- Projector
- Screen
- Birthday cake
- Plates
- Forks
- Napkins
- Knife
- Water/juice boxes
- Tablecloths
- Prizes
- Socks
- Brown yarn
- Glue

Budget

Approximately $50 for cake, refreshments, and prizes

General Comments

Depending how slowly tweens move through these activities, you may not have time to cover everything in one hour. You may choose to offer a longer program, or to divide the program into two parts. Additional information about hobbits and Hobbit Day is available online at Wikipedia: *http://en.wikipedia.org/wiki/Hobbit* and *http://en.wikipedia.org/wiki/Hobbit_Day*.

Oh, Sit: Library Edition! Extreme Musical Chairs

This is loosely based on the new television game show that is a wacky Japanese Game Show style. The idea is to fit in as many different variations of musical chairs as possible, including an obstacle course if you so choose. You can offer prizes for the winners, or just simply have tweens play for bragging rights. We save book donations that are new or like-new to hand out as prizes.

Program Advertisement

Are you prepared to go head-to-head in this obstacle-course style, hot-octane musical chair competition? Who will seize the last chair in this Extreme Musical Chairs battle?

Number of Spaces Available

20

Program Preparation (1 hour)

1. Decide what variations of musical chairs you will be offering.

2. Once you know approximately how many games you'll be playing, try to see if you can have prizes or make funny certificates or awards.

3. Pull current CDs to play for the music.

Room Set-up

As many chairs as there are participants

Create a small obstacle course if you have the space: include a mat, table to crawl under, tape on the ground to walk a tight rope, etc.

Program Outline

1. Icebreaker: Choose a great icebreaker from Chapter 3, or play Rain Pours for... musical chairs .

Variations of Musical Chairs:

Rain Pours for... is one of the variations, which means it needs to have the same size, style heading as Animal Musical Chairs.

Based on the game 'A Cold Wind Blows' in *The New Games Book*, edited by Andrew Fluegelman. You will need a set of chairs, with one less than the amount of players you have. Someone starts off as 'It'. In each round, 'It' calls out "Rain pours for. . ." and describes a characteristic of people in the group. Examples could be:

Rain pours for anyone wearing yellow!

Rain pours for red heads!

Rain pours for anyone in sixth grade!

Rain pours for whoever plays a sport!

Rain pours if your name begins with T!

All of the players for whom rain pours must leave their seat and find a new one, at the same time 'It' is also looking to steal a seat. When all the seats are taken, whoever is left standing is 'It' for the next round.

Animal Musical Chairs

You will need a set of chairs and music. Jungle music would be appropriate, but not necessary. You will need one less chair than participants.

Arrange the chairs in a circle or whatever shape fits yourspace.

Begin by playing the traditional way so they get a feel for musical chairs. Play music and when the music stops, everyone must scramble to find a chair. There will be one person who will not a get a chair. Usually they'd be out, but in this case they are 'It.'

Ask 'It' what their favorite animal is. Then ask 'It' how their favorite animal moves and sounds. For example, if 'It' claims that their favorite animal is a cat they would meow and crawl.

The remaining players must circle the chairs as 'It's' favorite animal, so in this case they would be imitating cats. Remove one chair so there is always one less chair than players. The next person who does not get a chair will have to state their favorite animal until only one stands. The sillier the animal, the better! The last person standing wins!

Extreme Musical Chairs

This is played the same way as your basic musical chairs except the DJ (the person controlling the music) also yells out a different way to circle the chairs each round. Examples include:

- hopping
- skipping
- crawling
- walking backwards
- eyes closed (be careful)
- arms linked
- pick a partner and must imitate that partner
- jumping up and down
- chorus line
- the options are endless!

As usual, the last person standing is the winner!

Stool Toad

Create a bunch of cards, half with pictures of stools (as in a stool that you sit on) and half the pictures with toads. Lay the cards on the ground (no chairs needed for this variation). There will be one less card laying on the ground than participants that you have. As the music plays, players hop from card to card in a safe manner. When the music stops, if the player is on a stool they must get on their hands and knees to create a stool. Those that land on toads must find a stool to (delicately) sit on. One person will be left out and they can decide to remove a stool or toad card. Continue playing these rounds until only one person is left!

Puzzle Chairs

Have as many chairs as there are players. Also have pictures from any old magazine cut in half like a jigsaw puzzle. One part of the picture is kept face down on a chair and another part is given to the player. When the music stops, the player must find their corresponding chair. You can play this so that whoever takes the longest is out, or you can play it so everyone wins and you scramble the puzzle again.

Do You Like Your Neighbors?

Have all but one person sitting in a circle in chairs. One player begins the game standing in the middle of the circle. This player approaches any player in the circle and asks the question: "Do you like your neighbors?" The seated player who's been asked can answer either "yes" or "no".

If the questioned player answers "no", then the players on either side of them need to stand up and switch places as quickly as possible. Meanwhile, the player who began in the middle of the circle is also trying to grab one of the seats.

If the questioned player answers "yes", then they have to state who they do not like. For example: "Yes, I like my neighbors but I don't like people who wear white socks." In this case, everyone in the circle who is wearing white socks has to get up and switch places. The player who began in the middle of the circle is also trying to get a seat at the same time. Whoever is left standing at the end of the mad dash will have to begin the questioning again.

Islands

This is a variation of basic musical chairs. Instead of chairs, you use newspaper or poster board spread randomly on the ground. The idea is that the players are stranded, and the newspaper represents an island. As the music plays, the marooned players move around the newspaper, but don't step onto it. When the music stops they rush to an island to survive. Count slowly to five to give the players a chance to step onto the newspaper. After each round, remove sheets of newspaper until, after several rounds, only one sheet is left. You'll have a great time as lots of players try to fit onto the one sheet of paper.

Obstacle Course Musical Chairs

This is one way you can crown an ultimate Musical Chair champion! Have one less chair than participants and put the chairs throughout the room in different places, some upside down. Put obstacles that participants will have to cross in order to get to the next chair, such as walking in a straight line of tape, crawling under a table, rolling on a mat, etc. Just like regular musical chairs: when the music stops, players must scramble to find a chair but complete the obstacles first. The last person standing is the extreme champion!

2. Play as many musical chair variations as possible.

3. Clean up.

Materials Used

- Chairs
- Prizes
- Tape
- Items in the library to use for obstacle course

Budget

$0-$30

General Comments

Be careful - musical chairs can get very wild! You'll want to make sure to have rest periods, or maybe a few quiet rounds between the big ones.

Mother-Daughter Book Club

A great time to start a book club is September, especially if your club chooses to take a break over the summer months. This book club is unique in that it brings tween girls and a female adult to the library together. Often it is a mother and daughter who attend, however you may find a grandmother, aunt, older sibling, or support worker who wishes to join the tween in her life. While a tween book club collection may be a bit more difficult to establish or justify than adult collections, it is well worth the investment. The Oshawa Public Libraries children's book club sets are now used by three separate book clubs, as well as external organizations. Since a Mother-Daughter Book Club program outline is a book in itself, this will provide only a brief overview of such a program. Additional and more in-depth writings are available online by Cindy Hudson at *http://motherdaughterbookclub.com/*.

Program Advertisement

Girls ages 9-12 along with a special female in their lives, take part in this unique hour-long book club.

Number of Spaces Available

10 tweens plus adults

Program Preparation (2 hours average)

1. Establish the day, time, and frequency of the book club. A one hour session per month is recommended, although, depending on the availability of the adults and the reading abilities of the tweens, you might consider bi-monthly (once every two months) meetings.

2. Determine how books will be obtained. Some libraries purchase a copy for each tween and allow them to keep it after the program. Other libraries choose to purchase ten copies of each book, keeping them together as a book club set, either for staff use only or as a circulating set for all patrons or other library systems. If your budget is more restricted, look for neighboring libraries that might inter-library loan book club sets. Or, if you are part of a larger library system with multiple branches, choose titles of which you already have ten copies. Another alternative is to require tweens to purchase or obtain their own copies of the book.

3. If you choose to purchase book club sets, determine circulation policies and procedures. This includes borrowing periods, how the sets will be catalogued and barcoded, how book club sets will be reserved by library staff, etc.

4. Select book club set titles. Each September, you may wish to select, plan, and announce monthly titles for the entire year, or you may wish to select, plan, and announce only several months in advance. To help select appropriate titles, pay attention to what tweens are borrowing, read new (and old) tween releases, or consult the many excellent books and websites dedicated to mother-daughter and tween book clubs, such as "12 Great Books for Mother-Daughter Book Clubs" at *http://www. bookbundlz.com/BBArticle.aspx?articleId=50* or *"Popular Mother Daughter Book Club Books"* at *http://www.goodreads.com/shelf/show/mother-daughter-book-club*. You may also wish to choose books which feature a strong female character, or that already have discussion questions available via the publisher's or author's website.

5. Determine a sign-up process for the book club. You may opt for open registration and then close it once all spaces are filled, keeping the same members month after month. Or, you may choose to keep registration open each month, distributing books on a first come, first serve basis. For the sake of continuity, it is sometimes best to maintain the same group month after month. If no-shows become a problem, suggest that if a tween misses two consecutive meetings, the spot will be given away. It is also helpful to place reminder calls before each meeting and to include a meeting schedule hand-out in each book.

6. For the initial meeting, you might want to encourage book club members to booktalk a book they read over the summer months. This will allow for the first meeting to be more of a meet and greet, and also give you a better indication of the reading level and interests of the book club members. At the end of the first meeting, the next month's book selection can be distributed. Include some discussion questions for tweens and adults to think of as they read. It typically works best if the book is checked out on the tween's library card, and the copy can then be shared by the tween and their special adult.

7. Read the selected title for next month and write discussion questions if none can be found online or via the publisher.

8. Find activities or crafts related to the book.

Recommended Titles for Mother Daughter Book Clubs

A variety of genres and reading levels have been included in this list. Your choices will depend largely on the interests of your tweens, as well as their reading levels. You may find it best to start with a shorter and easier title to gauge their response.

Author	Title
Margaret Peterson Haddix	*Among the Hidden*
Kate Jaimet	*Dunces Anonymous*
Sharon Creech	*Granny Torelli Makes Soup*
Katherine Hannigan	*Ida B*
Meg Cabot	*Moving Day (Allie Finkle's Rules for Girls)*
Shannon Hale	*Princess Academy*
Cynthia Lord	*Rules*
Patricia MacLachlan	*Sarah, Plain and Tall*
Jean Little	*Somebody Else's Summer*
Caroline Stellings	*The Contest*
Heather Vogel Frederick	*The Mother-Daughter Book Club*
Jeanne Birdsall	*The Penderwicks*
Kit Pearson	*The Sky is Falling*
Greg Mortenson/Sarah Thomson	*Three Cups of Tea (Young Reader's Edition)*
Robert Weston	*Zorgamazoo*

Mother-Daughter

Welcome to the Mother-Daughter Book Club, a place for children and a special female in their lives to meet and discuss great books!

Now that you are registered, you will be part of our club until June, or until you decide that the Mother-Daughter Book Club is no longer right for you.

However, if you miss more than 2 consecutive meetings without providing a reason, your space may be given away.

If you are unable to attend a meeting, please call and inform a staff member at the Legends Centre Branch at 905-579-6111, ext. 5800.

To make sure everyone has fun, here are a few guidelines:

- Let everyone speak
- Try not to interrupt
- Difference of opinion are welcome
- Read at least 30 pages even if you don't like the book, then let us know why you didn't like it
- Come to a meeting even if you haven't finished reading the book
- Have fun!

When you are reading a book, here are a few things to think about:

- What happens in the story and why does it happen?
- Have you ever experienced similar events in your life?
- Describe the personality traits of each character.
- What have you learned from reading this story?
- Do you like the ending and does it make sense?
- Did you enjoy this story? Why or why not?

Room Set-up

Everyone can sit around a large table(s), or to make tweens feel more comfortable, adults can sit in traditional chairs and tweens can sit on bean bag chairs or floor cushions. Tables and chairs may be required for crafts or activities.

Program Outline

1. Icebreaker: Some of the group may know each other, but some may be strangers. Ask the adults to introduce their tweens and the tweens to introduce their adults. It will be interesting to see what they have to say about each other! Then select an icebreaker from Chapter 3. Nametags are helpful for the first few sessions.

2. Snacks: It's always a good idea to provide snacks and refreshments at book club meetings. Nothing brings people together better than food! Consider serving juice and water, as well as coffee and tea for adults. If the budget is an issue, ask members if they would like to organize the refreshments in a pot-luck or rotating system.

3. Discussion of the Book: Start by asking tweens and adults if they liked the book and why. You may then delve into more specific questions. The facilitator can either ask the questions, or a fun alternative is to type the questions on slips of paper and randomly distribute them to tweens and adults as they come into the program room. This will give everyone time to formulate an answer and help to get the discussion rolling.

4. Activity: If tweens really liked a book, the discussion might be endless, but if the book was less of a hit, there will be time to fill. Offer a craft or activity that relates to the book's themes, characters, plot, or setting. If you have access to the Internet and a computer/laptop during the program, visit the author's website or search YouTube to find a book trailer or interview with the author. If you can't find anything, board games or circle games are always fun.

5. Book Display: If the book you just discussed is the first in a series, display other books in that series. You can also display other books by that author or read-alikes to the title.

6. Distribution of the Next Title: Booktalk the next title and check-out the books. Remind members of the next meeting date.

7. Clean up.

Materials Used

- Nametags
- Markers
- Snacks and refreshments
- Materials for crafts or activities
- Books

Budget

Approximately $15 per month for refreshments and any craft or activity supplies

General Comments

If the thought of running a monthly book club is overwhelming, or if resources are limited for the purchase of book club sets, consider offering one-time book discussions. This works especially well for books that everyone is talking about, such as *Twilight* and *The Hunger Games*. If you have a lot of male tween customers, you might consider offering a Father-Son Book Club. The same format will apply, however, titles can focus on strong male characters, rather than female characters. Non-fiction titles and graphic novels might also be more appealing to boys. A Parent-Child or Family Book Club is less gender discriminating, but it may be more challenging to find titles that will appeal to all.

Further Reading about Book Clubs

MAKING A BOOKMARK DURING MOTHER- DAUGHTER BOOK CLUB. COURTESY OF OSHAWA PUBLIC LIBRARIES.

Gelman, Judy. *The Kids' Book Club Book: Reading Ideas, Recipes, Activities, and Smart Tips for Organizing Terrific Kids' Book Clubs*. Tarcher, 2007.

Hudson, Cindy. *Book by Book: The Complete Guide to Creating Mother-Daughter Book Clubs*. Seal Press, 2009.

Little, Dawn. "Starting a Father/Son Book Club." *Book Bundlz*. http://www.bookbundlz.com/BBArticle.aspx? articleId=59.

Soltan, Rita. *Reading Raps: A Book Club Guide for Librarians, Kids, and Families*. Libraries Unlimited, 2006.

Chapter 13: October

October is a month when programming picks up a bit – tweens are getting used to schoolwork and extracurricular activities, and parents know when schedules are clear to register tweens for programs. Also, October has great programming opportunities. Halloween is so popular with this age group that all of the programs we display here have a haunted twist: Urban Legends, ZombieFest, Nursery Nightmares, and hosting a Haunted House at the library. We also introduce the American Library Association's WrestleMania® Reading Challenge, which is sponsored by Young Adult Library Services Association and WWE in an effort to get tweens and teens reading beyond Teen Read Week (usually held the third week of October each year). It's a busy, but fun, month!

Urban Legends

Urban legends, or modern folktales and stories that may or may not be true, have been around since the 1960s, but they are still extremely popular with tweens today. With all of the Halloween happenings this month, October is a great time to do this program! It keeps tweens on the edge of their seats and they really love to decide which Urban Legends are fact or fiction. There are many variations that you can implement at your location.

Program Advertisement

Eating Pop Rocks and drinking pop at the same time causes your stomach to explode. A company will give you $245 for every third person to whom you forward a certain e-mail. You've heard stories like these before, now is your chance to learn more about these Urban Legends, win prizes, and swap spooky stories at this fun event.

Legends have it that eating pop rocks and drinking soda will cause your stomach to explode. Learn more about Urban Legends & win prizes at this fun event!

Urban Legends
at the library

JOIN US:
Legends Centre Branch
Friday, October 10, 2008
7:00 PM to 8:00 PM
Jess Hann Branch
Wednesday, October 22, 2008
7:00 PM to 8:00 PM

Free registration at any branch
Snacks will be provided

OSHAWA
Public Libraries
far more than you expect

McLaughlin Branch
65 Bagot Street
L1H 1N2

Jess Hann Branch
199 Wentworth St. W.
L1J 6P4

Northview Branch
250 Beatrice St. E.
L1G 7T6

Legends Centre Branch
1661 Harmony Rd. N.
L1H 7K5

www.oshawalibrary.on.ca

905-579-6111

Number of Spaces Available

30 spaces

Program Preparation (2 hours)

1. To choose which Urban Legends you'd like to feature, visit "Urban Legends Reference Pages" at *http://www.snopes.com.*

2. Use Microsoft® PowerPoint to create a slideshow of the Urban Legends. A sample presentation is available online at *https://sites.google.com/site/thetweenscene/.*

3. If you do not already have whiteboards and dry-erase markers, go to a dollar store and get four or more.

Room Set-up

5 tables and as many chairs as participants

Program Outline

1. Icebreaker: You may have to explain what Urban Legends are, but once you do, the tweens can tell their favorite Urban Legend or scary story.

2. Formation of Teams: Divide tweens into teams of 3-4. Each team decides on a team name.

3. Explain the Rules:
   A. Follow directions.
   B. Work together as a team to decide if the Urban Legend is true or false.
   C. Write your answer on the provided whiteboards and reveal when instructed to do so.

4. Urban Legends Slide Show: The Slide Show can be as long or as short as you prefer. Keep track of which teams correctly answer each Urban Legend. Be prepared for challenges.

5. Announce the Winner: The winning team can pick out a prize.

6. Mad-Libs and Snacks: Mad-Libs is extremely popular with this age group. Keep it silly enough and the tweens will be rolling around with laughter. Make sure the snacks include the option of trying a few Pop Rocks with cola.

7. Urban Legends Quiz: If you have time, or need something to take up time, do an individual quiz that is similar to the Microsoft® Power Point, but on paper.

8. Award Prizes.

9. Clean up.

Materials Used

- Microsoft® PowerPoint
- Trivia sheets
- Dry-erase white boards
- Pop Rocks candy
- Cola
- Laptop/projector
- Snacks and beverages
- Prizes

Budget

Approximately $15 for supplies and snacks

General Comments

We've done this a few times now and it's always very popular. Watching the tweens share stories about their own experiences with Urban Legends is fun for the library staff, too! This is also a very popular class visit.

Zombiefest

Zombies are truly the new vampire! Undead is still cool and tweens love anything having to do with Zombies–especially tween boys!

Program Advertisement

Are you prepared for a Zombie attack? Make your own survival gear, become a zombie, win prizes, and more at this Zombie-tastic event!

Number of Spaces Available

20 spaces

Program Preparation (Time varies with number of chosen activities)

1. Decide which zombie-tastic events you'd like to have at your Zombiefest.

2. Create handouts and book displays.

3. Get face-paint.

4. Create cards with different decomposing and rotting body parts. Examples can include: Oozing Brain, Rotting Arm, Torn Finger, Decomposed Toe, Nobby Knee, Severed Hand, Torn Eyeball, etc.

5. Make a book display with zombie titles, such as *The Zombie Survival Guide: Complete Protection from the Living Dead* by Max Brooks; *Generation Dead* by Daniel Waters; *Pride and Prejudice and Zombies* by Seth Grahame-Smith; and *Forest of Hands and Feet* by Carrie Ryan.

6. Create a Graveyard Cake

Room Set-up

5 tables with as many chairs as participants

Program Outline

1. Introduction: Show the tweens the following zombie book trailers and tell them about the activities they will be doing during the program:
   A. *Pride and Prejudice and Zombies* by Seth Grahame-Smith and Jane Austen *http://www. youtube.com/watch?v=FzowFJTApfY*
   B. *The Forest of Hands and Teeth* by Carrie Ryan *http://www.youtube.com/ watch?v=ou1s3t6q2Q4*
   C. *Generation Dead* by Daniel Waters *http://gendead.com/#/video*

2. Icebreaker: "What Decomposing Body Part Am I?" As the tweens arrive, tape a body part card on each of their backs. By asking each other only yes/no questions, tweens must guess what body part is affixed to their back. Once they guess, they must find their matching body part (for example, a tween that has a decomposing leg must find another tween with same part).

3. Zombie Make-Up: Tweens paint their faces white, then complete the zombie look with dark circles under their eyes using black, gray, or dark green eye shadow, and adding blood with red face paint. For those tweens that would prefer not to wear make-up offer a paper mask craft. Print zombie faces (several are available at *http://www.freefunfings.com/masks/index.html*), cut out, attach strings, and wear.

4. Zombie Walk: Explain the basics of walking like a zombie. For example, lock your legs, pretend you have really heavy limbs, and maybe drag one foot behind. Do not walk in a straight line and make sure to let out a groan here and there. Practice walking like a zombie. You may even offer prizes for best zombie walk.

INGREDIENTS

- 2 cups all-purpose flour
- 2 cups sugar
- 1 teaspoon baking soda
- 1/2 teaspoon salt
- 1 cup butter
- 1 cup water
- 1/4 cup baking cocoa
- 1/2 cup sour cream
- 2 eggs

FROSTING:

- 1/4 cup butter
- 5 tablespoons milk
- 2 tablespoons baking cocoa
- 2 cups confectioners' sugar
- 1/2 teaspoon vanilla extract
- 18 cream-filled chocolate sandwich cookies
- Green and brown decorator's icing or gel
- 9 cream-filled oval vanilla sandwich cookies
- 1 cup whipped topping
- Pumpkin candies and gummy worms, optional

DIRECTIONS:

- In a bowl, combine flour, sugar, baking soda and salt and set aside.
- In a saucepan, combine butter, water and cocoa and bring it to a boil over medium heat. Once it is boiled add to flour mixture previously made and beat well. Beat in sour cream and eggs to the mixture.
- Pour the mixture into a greased 13" x 9" baking pan. Bake at 350° (F) for 35-38 minutes or until a toothpick inserted near the center comes out clean.
- Once baked, cool it on a wire rack for 5 minutes.
- Meanwhile, in a saucepan, combine butter, milk and cocoa and bring to a boil.
- Remove the saucepan from heat and stir in sugar and vanilla into the mixture.
- Pour the mixture over the warm cake.
- Crumble chocolate cookies and sprinkle over the still warm frosting.
- Cool the cake completely.
- For tombstones use icing to decorate vanilla cookies with words, faces or pictures. Place the cookies onto the cake.
- For ghosts, make mounds of whipped topping and use the icing to add eyes and mouths.
- Refrigerate the cake for at least 1 hour.
- Before serving the cake add pumpkins and gummy worms for that added special touch.
- Yields 16 servings.

BRIANNE PRACTICING HER ZOMBIE WALK. COURTESY OF OSHAWA PUBLIC LIBRARIES

5. Zombie and Humans Game: Mark two parallel lines on the floor using masking tape. Select one tween to be the zombie and divide the remaining tweens into two groups to be the humans. Place the zombie in between the lines and the humans outside of the lines (one group of humans should be on each side). When the zombie groans, all of the humans must try to run from one line to the other. The zombie must zombie walk/shuffle between the lines and try to tag the humans. If humans get tagged, they become decomposing zombies. They must drop to their knees and try to tag humans from the ground (they must remain on their knees and can only move their upper bodies). Repeat until the last person remains standing. He or she will have the title of Zombie Apocalypse Survivor.

6. Zombie Marco Polo Game: Select one tween to be the zombie and blindfold him or her. The zombie must zombie walk (as zombies do not run) with his or her hands outstretched and try to tag the other tweens. When the zombie groans, all of the other tweens must groan back and outstretch their arms. If a tween gets tagged, he or she becomes the zombie in the next game.

7. Zombie Flee and Hide Game: Mark a line on the floor, separating the room into two areas. Designate one person to lead the game. The rest of the tweens stand on the line facing the leader. When the leader yells "Flee!" all tweens run to the right side of the line. When the leader yells "Hide!" all the tweens should jump and crouch (as if hiding) to the left side of the line. When the leader groans, all tweens should groan and outstretch their arms. When the leader yells any other words, tweens should *not* move. If a tween makes an incorrect move, he or she is out of the game.

8. Zombie Voodoo Doll Craft: Now everyone can have a zombie in their house. This is an easy, but fun craft, and the tweens get to walk out of the program with a little zombie to call their own. You can find several string doll tutorials at *https://sites.google.com/site/libraryprogramideas/tweens-teens/string-dolls*.

9. Snacks: Serve a graveyard cake.

10.   Clean up.

Materials Used

- Laptop/projector
- Cards with body parts
- Masking tape
- Halloween make-up
- Supplies for zombie doll craft
- Snacks and beverages
- Prizes

Budget

Approximately $35 for supplies and snacks

General Comments

Zombies are not only popular in October – zombie themed programs have worked any time of the year for us! So far, the tweens haven't gotten tired of Tiffany's favorite joke – what does the vegetarian zombie eat? GRRRAAAAINS!

Nursery Nightmares

In this program, we'll actually encourage tweens to make babies—by make, we mean CRAFT, of course! Boys and girls both really enjoy this program because they get a chance to be a bit morbid and gory with their creations. Tweens love craft apocalypse programs; they really can be done year round!

Program Advertisement

Create your own little bloodsucker that is rotten to the core but oh-so-cute! This is not your ordinary nursery. Decide if you'd like to create a baby vamplet, mini-mummy, zombie cub, werewolf nipper or a creation of your own madness! You'll even get to create an undead certificate for your new devilish baby.

Number of Spaces Available

20 spaces

Program Preparation (Time varies with number of chosen activities)

1. Familiarize yourself with the different dolls that tweens can create. You can find several string doll tutorials at *https://sites.google.com/site/libraryprogramideas/tweens-teens/string-dolls.*

2. Ask for donations or purchase slightly used stuffed animals and/or action figures from thrift stores.

3. Set up a few tables with all the craft supplies you collect: yarn, styrofoam balls, glue, pipe cleaners, teddy bears, action figures, brass fasteners, studs, the sky is the limit!

Undead Certificate

Date of Death: _____

Full Name: _____

Belongs To: _____

Signature: _____

COURTESY OF OSHAWA PUBLIC LIBRARIES GRAPHICS DEPARTMENT>

Room Set-up

5 tables with as many chairs as participants

1 table full of craft supplies

Program Outline

1. Icebreaker: See Chapter 3 for great Icebreaker ideas. You could always have the tweens introduce themselves and name their favorite horror character.

2. Introduction: In this program tweens can create whatever kind of little monster they'd like! A great way of doing this is a string doll. Another fun way is by taking a doll that's already made, like a stuffed animal or action figure, and making it look all gory and monstrous.

3. Have tweens create/fill out their Undead Certificate.

4. Clean up.

Materials Used

- Craft supplies
- Snacks and beverages
- Undead certificate
- Prizes

Budget

Approximately $35 for supplies and snacks

General Comments

Here's a tip for the string doll head: a faster way to make the head is to start off with a small Styrofoam ball as the base and wrap string around that. Stick a pipe cleaner into the Styrofoam ball for the body!

Haunted Library

Everyone loves a haunted house, especially one that takes place in the library! This is a unique program because it is an all-ages event that is not exclusive to tweens. There can be a lot of tween involvement if it is run by members of the tween interest group (TWIG) and/or teen advisory board (TAB). If your library does not host such groups, staff members may also run the program. Be prepared to recruit a lot of bodies for set-up, clean-up, and to ensure the program runs smoothly. Haunted Library is a very versatile program and can reflect a variety of themes. Each year, our TWIG and TAB groups choose the theme, which helps to provide creative direction and to give the all-ages participants a thrilling experience! Changing the theme also encourages participants to return year after year in anticipation of new and exciting elements. Theme examples include haunted hospital and haunted circus.

Program Advertisement

Do you know what happens in the library when the lights go out? Enter our haunted house to find the answer! An all-ages program. Children under the age of 8 must be accompanied by an adult. Drop-in event.

Number of Spaces Available

Variable; as many as can go through the haunted house in the designated time frame. It will also depend on the size of your haunted house. We could permit a group of ten people to enter the haunted house approximately every ten minutes.

Program Preparation (3-4 hours)

1. We meet with our TWIG and TAB for ideas starting at the beginning of September and create a floor plan, lay-out, and general theme. Our themes have included: Haunted Library, Haunted Hospital, Haunted Movie Theatre, Haunted Circus, and Haunted Wedding. We then make a list of props, costumes, and more that we will need in order to have the house run successfully. Many props are found around the home and library, although we buy quite a bit from the dollar store. We put about eight hours of planning into the house itself, and then set-up takes about three to four hours, depending on how elaborate you'd like it to be and how many helpers you have.

2. Print a color-coded numbering system to hand to participants as they arrive. For example, the numbers 1 through 10 printed on 10 different colours of cardstock. If you are going to re-use these numbers you might laminate them.

3. Print a variety of Halloween-themed coloring pages, mazes, word searches, crossword puzzles, and other activities to entertain those waiting in the reception area.

4. Schedule your helpers to arrive at a certain time to decorate according to the lay-out plan. Make sure everyone knows their roles--some will be part of the Haunted House (ghosts, monsters, fortune tellers, etc.), while some will be tour guides--those who guide the Haunted House visitors with a flashlight. Decorate and set-up and then serve the volunteers pizza while they get ready for the Haunted House to begin. Make sure you do a few dress rehearsals, so you can work out any kinks!

Room Set-up

In the reception area, set-up tables and chairs for those waiting to enter the haunted house. In addition to coloring stations, you can set up a snack and refreshment table. Play Halloween-themed music or show a Halloween-themed video.

The house can be set up according to the space you have. We had a large auditorium, so we created a tunnel out of tables, utilized a stage area for a graveyard, covered the walls in garbage bags, used tables as room dividers, and depending on the theme, set up different areas of the house. We dim the lights and play spooky music – a CD soundtrack that the library owns. The dollar stores usually carry them.

Program Outline

1. Number Distribution: The easiest way to move people through the haunted house is in small groups. We recommend 8-10 per group, or even fewer if your haunted house space is small. As participants arrive, ask how many are in their party. Many times a family or group of friends will want to tour the haunted house together. Hand each guest a color-coded number, keeping parties together. For example, a family of 4 would be given numbers 1-4 purple, a group of 3 friends would be given numbers 5-7 purple, a family of 3 would be given numbers 8-10 purple. Move on to the next color for the next group of participants. If you only have 2 spaces left in one color set and a group of 3 arrives, you will want to assign them to the next color set, but still try to fill the previous 2 spots if a group of 2 arrive later. Generally people will be understanding of group sizes and restrictions.

2. Reception Area Activities: While participants are waiting to enter the haunted house, they may work on activity sheets, watch a video, enjoy refreshments, or partake in any other activities you organize. Depending on your turn-out, some guests may have to wait up to thirty minutes or more. That's why these activities are important.

3. The Tour Begins: Once participants start to arrive and the TWIG and TAB members are ready, the tours can begin. Call the first number grouping forward. For example, purple 1 through 10. Once all of the participants with those numbers step forward, have the tour guide collect the tickets and escort the first group through the haunted house. Repeat approximately every ten minutes. A good rule of thumb is to allow the first group to get half-way through the haunted house before allowing the second group to enter. Also be sure to ask tour guides to return the numbers to the reception area for re-distribution as more participants arrive. Have some blank card-stock on hand to re-write any numbers that become lost or damaged.

4. The Tour through the House: Be prepared for crying. As soon as some children enter the area and see it is dark and hear scary music, they immediately burst into tears. Many children love to be scared, but some really hate it, or are being forced in by their parents. Have the tour guide explain what's happening and use a flashlight to guide the way. On the way out, we provide candy, popcorn, and glowsticks--freebies for all participants.

5. Clean up: This part is exhausting! Depending on your location, you might be able to save the clean up for another day. Try to keep your volunteers cheery and revved up so the cleaning goes as quickly and as smoothly as possible!

Materials Used

- Colored cardstock for numbering system
- Coloring/worksheets, crayons, pencils, Halloween-themed music and/or video for reception area
- Snacks and juice for reception area
- Flashlights for tour guides
- Garbage bags for wall covering
- Tape
- Halloween decorations
- Sound system, sounds effects recording
- Scissors
- Costumes

Budget

Your expenses will vary greatly, depending on the size of your haunted house and how many materials are available to you for free. Consider asking staff members to loan their personal decorations. Ask TWIG and TAB members to provide their own costumes. Thrift stores and dollar stores also offer great decorations for discounted prices. If you know that you'd like to offer this program next

October, take advantage of heavily discounted clearance items after Halloween. Remember that any initial purchases can be used year after year (as long as they hold up to the wear and tear of set-up, take-down, and storage). If you have a limited budget, you may want to opt out of serving beverages or snacks.

General Comments

Haunted Library has now been popular for four consecutive years at Oshawa Public Libraries and the crowds just keep coming! It is not unusual for this event to draw nearly 250 people. If your event gets stale at one location, try re-locating it to another branch the following year, as this will draw a whole new audience. From our experience, local radio and newspaper coverage has been outstanding with many live-on-location broadcasts and print ads. Depending on how dark and scary you make your haunted house, be prepared for some little ones (and even older ones) to decide not to go in. Before each tour begins, make it clear that people can leave at any time and encourage them to re-visit the reception area to partake in some tamer fun.

HANGING OUT AFTER A BUSY DAY AT THE HAUNTED HOUSE. COURTESY OF OSHAWA PUBLIC LIBRARIES GRAPHICS DEPARTMENT.

YALSA WrestleMania® Reading Challenge

If your library doesn't participate in the annual YALSA WrestleMania Reading Challenge, you should jump on this bandwagon as soon as possible! We have been lucky enough to have sent three tweens to WrestleMania in the past. The WrestleMania Reading Challenge is sponsored by YALSA and World Wrestling Entertainment. The program encourages teens and tweens to read during Teen Read Week and beyond, especially catering to non-traditional library users and readers. By doing so, they can win prizes donated by WWE and other organizations, including tickets to WrestleMania and $2,000 for their library. It's easy to participate – just register on the YALSA website *http://www.ala.org/yalsa/teenreading/wrmc/wrmc*. Register and get your participants to complete the task YALSA requests – in the past it's been creating a bookmark or writing a letter to a favorite wrestler convincing him or her to read a certain book. Then you pick the best ones to submit and wait to hear from YALSA if any of your participants were picked! It's super fun and a great way to promote reading.

Chapter 14: November

The weather outside may be dull and dark as winter plans it's approach, but inside, the library is awash with glitter and sparkles. November may be a slower programming month as family celebrations and early holiday festivities kick into high gear, taking up more of the tweens' time than usual. But if you offer extra-fabulous programs, it will be hard for them to stay away! What is more fabulous than an un-birthday party, a crazy game show, glittery body art, and a celebration of a famous boy band? A fabulous library to act as host!

Merry Unbirthday to You!

Based on Lewis Carroll's *Through the Looking-Glass,* this program allows guests to celebrate their very own unbirthdays! What is an unbirthday? Any day that is not your birthday.

Program Advertisement

A very merry unbirthday to you! You'll be mad as the hatter in this non-stop fun event that celebrates *everyone's* birthday!

Number of Spaces Available

30 spaces (depending on materials)

Program Preparation (1 hour)

1. Prepare Mad Hatter hat craft

2. Obtain cupcakes (either make or buy).

3. Prepare loot bags—birthday bags with small prizes from the dollar store.

4. Decorate room as if you were decorating for a birthday party.

5. For inspiration, look online: *http://www. suite101.com/content/how-to-throw-an-un-birthday-party-a210089*.

Room Set-up

5 tables with 6 chairs around each

Program Outline

1. Icebreaker: Since this program has an *Alice in Wonderland* theme, have the tweens introduce themselves and name their favorite character from *Alice in Wonderland*.

2. Mad Hatter Hat Craft: It's quite simple to make a giant hat out of a paper bag. Before constructing and rolling the hat, have tweens decorate the hat in any way that they'd like. See side bar for full directions.

How to Make a Mad Hatter Hat
Materials:
Paper bag
Tissue paper
Masking tape
Double-sided tape
Index card
Markers
Decals, stickers

Instructions:
Decorate the bag however you'd like. Crumple up some tissue and put inside the paper bag. Roll up edges of bag and secure with masking tape if needed. The roll is your brim. If the brim is too big, keep rolling until it fits your head. It will immediately look like a Mad Hatter hat, especially if you tuck in the edges.! Grab an index card and write your own version of Mad Hatter numbers and tape it on the brim.

3. Riddle Me This
    - Either during the creation of the hats or after, ask tweens riddles. Help them to come up with the answers.
    - Ask tweens to share any riddles they know.
    - Use the Mad Hatter's favorite line, "Why is a raven like a writing desk?" (There is no answer.)

4. Let Them Eat Cake: Cupcakes are perfect for this event because everyone gets their own and you can have different flavors. If you prefer, you can serve regular cake. If allowed, light birthday candles and sing, "Happy Birthday, not me!"

5. Make a Birthday Present or Card: Get creative! The tweens make their own birthday present (Modge Podging a picture frame or make badges with a button maker) or they can make each other unbirthday cards. During this time you can read from *Alice in Wonderland* or show one of the movies, if you have a movie license.

6. Hand out loot bags.

7. Clean up.

Materials Used

- Paper bags
- Markers
- Paper cut-outs/decals
- Masking tape
- Double sided tape
- Glue
- Construction paper
- Cupcakes
- Birthday candles
- Lighter/matches
- Birthday party tablecloths
- Loot bags
- Trinkets for loot bags
- Materials needed for craft
- Snacks and beverages

Budget

Approximately $40 for supplies and snacks

General Comments

Our program was scheduled soon after the release of the Tim Burton version of *Alice in Wonderland*, so we put a gothic twist on things in Tim Burton fashion. Some libraries love to have this program as a tea party, in true Mad Hatter fashion. You can also have it be a bit more cartoon-y or more focused on the literature. It's all about what you think your tweens would enjoy!

Henna or Glitter Tattoos

Tweens can use henna to express themselves with body art in a way that is not permanent. You can buy a kit and try to be your own henna artist, or you can check in your community to see if there is someone who does henna at a reasonable price. We have a henna artist in our community who also specializes in glitter tattoos. Both art forms are not permanent; henna lasts up to three weeks, while the glitter tattoos last as long as any temporary tattoo.

Program Advertisement

Learn the ancient art of henna at this exciting event. Artist _____ will be creating free, safe, temporary henna tattoos for you! A signed parent/guardian permission form must be returned prior to the workshop.

Get inked at the library – temporarily, of course! The latest fashion craze from Europe will be offered at Oshawa Public Libraries for free! Participants under 18 will need to have a permission slip filled out ahead of time. The glitter tattoos are temporary, non-toxic, and last 3-13 days depending on placement.

Number of Spaces Available

This depends on your materials or how much time you have – normally, we can accommodate 25 people in 1 hour

Program Preparation

1. Decide if you are doing the henna yourself or locating an artist. If hiring an artist, check references. If doing the henna yourself or allowing the tweens to do it, shop for supplies.

2. Prepare materials. For a list of materials and how to run the program without a henna artist, visit RoseMary Honnold's site *http://www.rhonnold.com/mehndi.html.*

3. Print as many numbers as there are participants for taking turns.

4. Pull any books the library may have that contain information about henna or body modification.

5. Print henna designs and examples.

Room Set-up

1 table with 2 chairs for the henna/glitter tattoo station
Enough chairs set up for participants who will be waiting

Program Outline

1. Assign Numbers: As the tweens arrive, assign each a number.

2. Icebreaker: Choose a favorite from Chapter 3.

3. Explain how the henna or glitter tattoos work.

4. Begin event: When a tween's number is called, it is his or her turn for henna or a glitter tattoo. While they are waiting, they can pick out their designs or work on puzzles and board games.

5. Clean up.

Materials Used

- Henna tattoo materials
- Glitter tattoo materials

- Puzzles
- Paper for numbers
- Beverages
- Books about henna or body modification

Budget

This depends on if you have an outside artist come to your library or if you buy all the materials yourself. For the artist that our library books, it is about $150 a session. Henna is inexpensive to buy and you can always have the tweens pick a partner and do designs on each other.

General Comments

We have done this program with and without permission slips. The permission slips are a formality and can save you in the end if a tween shows up to this event not realizing the henna design will last up to three weeks. Also, if any of your participants attend private school, they may not be allowed to have designs anywhere that is visible, as it does not meet uniform requirements. You can always offer this program in the summer because of school rules.

Minute to Win It

At this writing, *Minute to Win It* is a very popular game show. Their challenges are easy to duplicate and they even give you ideas on their website which is available at *http://www.nbc.com/minute-to-win-it/how-to/*. Teachers, stores, scouts, gyms, and other groups use these challenges. The challenges are fun and once you have created them for one program, you can always use them as part of another program.

Program Advertisement

You have one minute to complete crazy tasks with household products! Will you be up to the task? You only have one minute to win it!

Number of Spaces Available

30 spaces

Program Preparation (3 to 4 hours)

1. It helps to watch *Minute to Win It* in order to understand how the concept works if you are not familiar.

2. Decide which games you are going to have the contestants try. Visit NBC's listing for list of *Minute to Win It* games at *http://www.nbc.com/minute-to-win-it/how-to/*.

3. Collect any items and construct any devices you may need for game play.

4. Print the names of the games and cut out. The tweens will draw these out of a hat.

5. If you do not understand how a game works, there are many videos online.

Room Set-up

7 tables with games (fully labeled) laid out

Program Outline

1. Icebreaker: The tweens introduce themselves and name their favorite game show.

2. Game Play: The tweens can compete individually or as partners. Follow the same structure as the TV show – a game is drawn and they have one minute to complete the challenge. If you have time, allow players three one minute chances.

3. Award Prizes: Award prizes for tweens who can complete a challenge. You may also want to have consolation prizes on hand for those that do not complete a challenge but still had fun!

4. Clean up.

Materials Used

- Paper
- Markers
- Pens
- Scissors
- Stopwatch or clock
- Materials for the challenges you've picked
- Snacks
- Beverages
- Prizes

Budget

Approximately $25 for food and prizes – all other materials were in-house.

General Comments

Some challenges are much harder than they look. For fun factor, the tweens might find it hilarious for YOU to try some of the challenges – go ahead and give it a try.

EXCITED AFTER COMPLETING SOME CRAZY TASKS AT MINUTE TO WIN IT. COURTESY OF OSHAWA PUBLIC LIBRARIES GRAPHICS DEPARTMENT.

One Direction (1D) FanFest

It seems that every year, a new tween heart throb breaks onto the stage, creating pandemonium and "fan-demonium" everywhere! In the spotlight right now is British/Irish boy band One Direction, better known to their fans as 1D. With a huge 2014 worldwide tour, over 17 million Twitter followers, and a handful of music awards, 1D was duly named Billboard's Top New Artist of 2012. If you haven't been following the hype, the boys of 1D (Zayn, Niall, Liam, Louis, and Harry) came together on the hit UK television show, The X-Factor. After the show, their success continued to rise, leaving countless 1D fans talking about their favorite boys. These "Directioners," as they call themselves, certainly have "One Direction infection" and will be super excited to see a fanfest at their local library! To learn more about One Direction, visit their official website *http://www.onedirectionmusic.com*.

Program Advertisement

Calling all "Directioners!" Are you a huge fan of Zayn, Niall, Liam, Louis, and Harry? Do you know all of the lyrics to "What Makes You Beautfiul?" Celebrate the British boy band One Direction and unite with other fans in this fun-filled fanfest party! For tweens ages 10-14.

Number of Spaces Available

30

Program Preparation (2hours)

1. Find or make a microphone.

2. Borrow a One Direction CD from the collection, or download their music from *www.itunes.com*.

3. Purchase a One Direction poster. For online shopping, try *www.allposters.com*. Or, find a picture of the band online and enlarge as needed.

4. Print and/or cut out a pair of sunglasses, sized to match the poster.

5. Print copies of the One Direction trivia reproducible.

6. Using any word processing or graphics program, design a One Direction bingo card for each tween. Be sure to mix-up the order on each card.

Room Set-up

Tables and chairs for crafts

An open area for games

Program Outline

1. Icebreaker: Ask each tween to say their name and favorite One Direction band member.

Ideas for bingo card images:
- 1D (the word)
- Zayn
- Niall
- Liam
- Louis
- Harry
- British flag
- X-Factor (the word)
- Microphone
- Heart
- Shamrock
- Telephone booth
- CD
- Map of Great Britain
- Guitar
- Piano
- One Thing (words)
- Up All Night (words)
- Beautiful (the word)
- Directioner (the word)
- Music symbols
- A bowtie

2, Pass the Microphone: This game is similar to "Hot Potato." Have tweens pass a real microphone (from a karaoke machine or PA system), or a homemade microphone (a paper towel tube with balled up aluminum foil at the top) from one person to the next. Play One Direction's music while this is happening, stopping the music at random intervals. If a tween is holding the microphone when the music stops, s/he is out. Continue until only one tween is left, crowning them the winner.

3, Pin the Sunglasses on One Direction: This game is similar to "Pin the Tail on the Donkey." Place a One Direction poster on the wall and have tweens take turns wearing a blindfold and pinning paper sunglasses on their favorite band member. Have tweens say the name of their intended target before taking their turn.

4. One Direction Word Art: Give each tween two sheets of construction paper, preferably a larger size or cut from a roll. Draw the number "1" on the first page and the letter "D" on the second page, using block lettering for both. Cut out each image and decorate using pictures of One Direction band members (from magazines or the Internet), words (such as "One Direction" "Liam," or "What Makes You Beautiful"), One Direction stickers (available at *www.amazon.com*), or any other craft supplies you have in your cupboard.

So you love One Direction?????

Let's see how much you really know about your favorite band!

1. Which television show did the boys get their start on?
2. What magazine named One Direction the Top New Artist of 2012?
3. Which country music singer did Harry Styles date?
4. Complete the lyric: "Baby you light up my world like _____."
5. Guess the song title: tiny items.
6. Who is the oldest member of One Direction?
7. In what month was Zayn born?
8. Is Niall left-handed or right-handed?
9. Which band member had a kidney removed when he was a kid?

Bonus: In which three countries was "Up All Night" recorded?

Answers:

1. The X-Factor
2. Billboard
3. Taylor Swift
4. Nobody else
5. Little Things
6. Louis
7. January
8. Left-handed
9. Liam

Bonus: UK, US, Sweden

5. One Direction Trivia: Have copies of the trivia sheet available for tweens who finish their craft early.

6. One Direction Bingo: Play a game of bingo, but have tweens call "One Direction" instead of bingo.

7. One Direction Musical Chairs: This is the same as everyone's favorite childhood game, except One Direction music is played. Place chairs in a circle, facing out, with one less chair than there are people. When the music stops, everyone must find a seat. The person left standing is out. Remove a chair and repeat until only one person is left with a seat.

8. Snacks: Serve a cake, cupcakes or cookies that have "1D" written on them in icing.

9. Clean up.

Materials Used

- Microphone or a paper towel tube and aluminum foil
- CD player/MP3 player
- One Direction CD or MP3s
- One Direction poster
- Sticky tack
- Paper sunglasses
- Blindfold
- Construction paper
- Scissors
- Markers
- One Direction images, stickers
- Other craft supplies for decorating
- Bingo chips
- Cake, cupcakes or cookies
- Tubes of icing

Budget

Approximately $20

General Comments

Even though this is a One Direction themed party, it can easily be adapted to celebrate any musician or band. In fact, this same program outline was used when Hannah Montana/Miley Cyrus was the most trending tween artist. This format seems to work well, even if the activities seem a bit juvenile. As long as their favorite band is involved, tweens really don't care what the activities are. One last note: for the most part, only girls will register for these types of programs, as the bands typically cater to females audiences. Don't be surprised if the occasional boy registers though!

Chapter 15: December

Wow – a full year of programming has gone by! Holiday break at school may bring more tweens to your library than usual, so you'll want to have some stellar programming options for them to try. In December, you do not have to rely on holiday-related programming; although it's fun to make gifts and holiday crafts, there are always other options. The four that have been popular at our library are: CSI at the Library, Party Like It's 1999, Cash Cab at the Library, and Neon New Year's Eve Party. With the exception of the last one, any of these programs can be offered any time of the year.

CSI at the Library

Tweens in our area really love *CSI* television shows and this program has been popular; we've hosted it several times. Other library systems ask about this program more than any other. It's a fun spin on your basic murder mystery and you can keep it simple, or make it as elaborate as you like.

Program Advertisement

Do you have what it takes to solve a crime scene mystery? Think it's as easy as it looks on TV? Come and find out how good a detective you are!

Number of Spaces Available

30 spaces

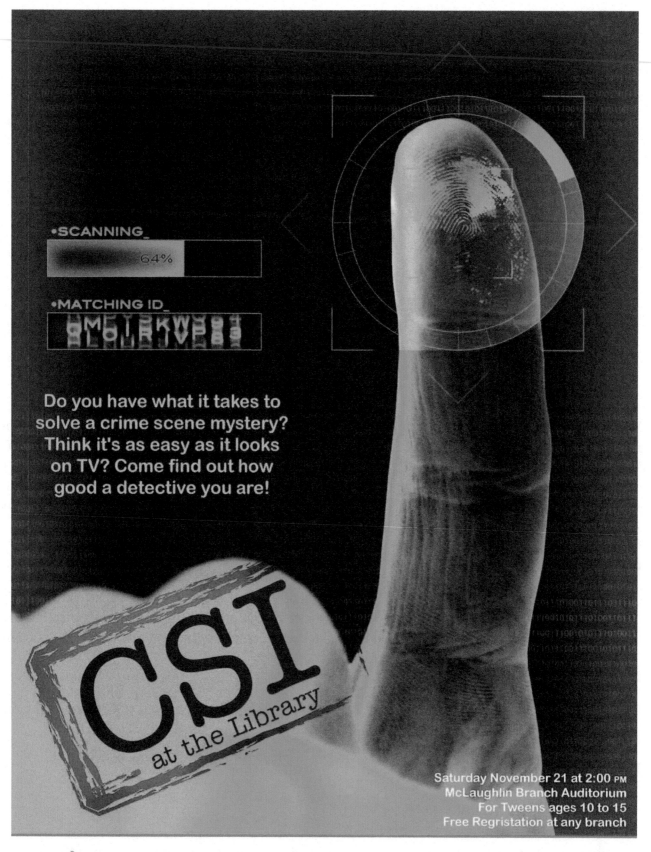

•SCANNING_

64%

•MATCHING ID_

Do you have what it takes to solve a crime scene mystery? Think it's as easy as it looks on TV? Come find out how good a detective you are!

CSI
at the Library

Saturday November 21 at 2:00 PM
McLaughlin Branch Auditorium
For Tweens ages 10 to 15
Free Regristation at any branch

OSHAWA
Public Libraries
far more than you expect

McLaughlin Branch	Jess Hann Branch	Northview Branch	Legends Centre Branch
65 Bagot Street	199 Wentworth St. W.	250 Beatrice St. E.	1661 Harmony Rd. N.
L1H 1N2	L1J 6P4	L1G 7T6	L1H 7K5

www.oshawalibrary.on.ca   905-579-6111

COURTESY OF OSHAWA PUBLIC LIBRARIES GRAPHICS DEPARTMENT

Program Preparation (3 hours)

1. Create your storyline. If your creative juices are not flowing, there are many murder mysteries online or you can use ours. Check it out at: *https://sites.google.com/site/thetweenscene/home/december-1* or *https://sites.google.com/site/libraryprogramideas/murder-mysteries.* Here is a list of games without murders: *http://www.whodunnitmysteries.com/games_no_murder.html.* To familiarize yourself with *Crime Scene Investigation,* visit: *http://en.wikipedia.org/wiki/CSI:_Crime_Scene_Investigation.*

2. Print out your files and witness statements. If you're using our storyline, these are available at *https://sites.google.com/site/thetweenscene/home/december-1.*

3. Obtain "evidence" and print out "finger prints" and "DNA." Once you decide what kind of evidence you'll be using, get your hands on them by asking co-workers, etc. We used a baseball bat, water bottles, a weight, a paint brush, and other items that suited our story.

4. Decide if you're going to involve "actors" (e.g. staff members who are willing to be interviewed).

Room Set-up

Three tables for *CSI* labs

Taped off areas for weapons and DNA evidence

An area for prizes, ours were books

Program Outline

1. Icebreaker: Choose a favorite from Chapter 3.

2. Go Over Rules:
    A. No running.
    B. Stay with your team.
    C. Be quiet so you don't give other teams your secrets.

2. Assign up to eight teams; teams separate and make a *CSI* team name, pick a lead detective, and pick a secretary detective.

3. Give each team a case file; have them go over it for about eight to ten minutes to see if there are any questions.

4. Teams find the possible murder weapon; bring it to one of the crime labs in their district (tables set up by librarians). If it is the right weapon for their team, give them their clue (a fingerprint) that corresponds with their color.

5. Now the teams have to search water bottles and cups for DNA evidence and bring their cup or water bottle to one of the crime labs in their district.

6. If it is the right evidence, the team receives their statements from witnesses.

7. The team is instructed to quietly pick a place in the auditorium to go over the statements so everyone knows what is going on, and decide who they think it is based on speculation. The secretary writes this suspect's name down.

8. Once they have a suspect, give the team a suspect statement.

9. After reading the suspect statement, they write down who they think the murderer is.

10. Tweens receive their clues and prove their theory with clues: They turn over the statements and compare the fingerprints and DNA of their suspect to the evidence they found to see if it is a match. If it isn't, they must pick another suspect.

11. When the team is finished, they report to the head *CSI* headquarters for accolades. They get to pick out a book prize if they are one of the first two teams done.

12. When they have picked out a book, they can munch on snacks and discuss their findings with others who are finished.

Materials Used

- Witness statements
- Suspect statements
- Murder weapon (we used a baseball bat and various other items found around the library)
- Masking tape
- Clue cards
- Snacks if warranted
- Books (for prizes)

Budget

The books were donated and/or came out of the book budget. Snacks or costumes are an additional expense.

General Comments

A murder mystery may be too edgy for some communities. You can always have another kind of mystery, such as the stolen book cart or something equally as fun! We tried to keep ours with a *CSI* teen noir feel.

Party Like It's 1999

We hosted this event as a response to our tweens wanting to participate in things normally considered childish – coloring contests, story times, easier crafts, etc. They had asked, "Why should the pre-schoolers have all the fun? We want to play with the parachute, too!" When we created this program in 2010, we figured that our tweens were very young in 1999, so that's how we came up with the name. You may wish to change the date in the title to reflect your audience--Party Like It's 20__!

Program Advertisement

Remember how easy life was ten years ago, back when all you wanted to do was finger paint and play games? Well, you're never too old for that! Go back in time for just one day! Try finger painting, play Twister, participate in a coloring contest, and build your own ice cream sundae.

Number of Spaces Available

30 spaces

Program Preparation (1 ½ hours)

1. Obtain food for ice cream sundaes.

2. Print character coloring sheets that the tweens may have enjoyed when they were three or four years old. Ideas include TeleTubbies, Arthur, and SpongeBob.

3. Decide what book you'd like to read for story-time. We chose several Eric Carle books because we had a felt board to accompany them.

4. Select music that was popular when the tweens were young.

5. Gather other games you might play (parachute games, Twister, Duck Duck Goose).

Room Set-up

5 tables with 6 chairs around each

Ice cream sundae station

Program Outline

1. Icebreaker: Choose a favorite from Chapter 3.

2. Get Your Sillies Out: After the icebreaker, lead the tweens through an activity that would normally be done for pre-schoolers to get the sillies out. Usually we dance to Raffi's "Shake Your Sillies Out." More details on how to do this is available online at *http://youtu.be/Jh5VXLM2TLI.* Then direct tweens to play games that have been set out. If you are doing parachute play, you may want to dedicate this time to that.

3. Finger Painting: We provided safe non-toxic finger paints and the tweens *loved* getting messy. Award silly prizes for the best painting, most creative, messiest, etc. You can also do a coloring contest with your coloring sheets.

4. Make Your Own Sundae Station: What is more exciting than an ice cream station? Not much! Be sensitive to food allergies (nuts) and diabetes (sugar). As the tweens munch on their sundaes, you can play a movie, listen to music, or just have conversation.

5. Clean up.

Materials Used

- Felt board
- Picture books
- Board games
- Parachute
- Finger paints
- Coloring pages
- Crayons
- Paper
- Ice cream
- Ice cream toppings
- Paper bowls
- Napkins
- Spoons
- Tablecloths
- Beverages
- Prizes

Budget

Approximately $45 for supplies and snacks

General Comments

If this doesn't seem like enough planned to keep the tweens interested, here are more options – bring out the Play-doh, play "Mother, May I?" or "Red Light, Green Light."

PARTYING LIKE IT'S 1999 WITH SOME BOARD GAMES. COURTESY OF OSHAWA PUBLIC LIBRARIES GRAPHICS DEPARTMENT.

Cash Cab at the Library

Tweens may not watch this show, but their parents do! It's a fun spin on your basic trivia challenge with fun or silly prizes.

Program Advertisement

There are 13,000 cabs in the city but only one pays YOU! Try your best at our trivia and get a chance to win prizes.

Number of Spaces Available

30 spaces

Program Preparation (1 to 2 hours)

1. Buy play money or borrow from board games, such as Monopoly.

2. Find trivia. Make sure it's not too hard, and that it covers many different subjects. Some great trivia sites are located online at: *https://sites.google.com/site/libraryprogramideas/trivia* and *http://www. funtrivia.com/quizzes/for_children/index.html*.

3. Obtain candy or other prizes.

4. Familiarize yourself with *Cash Cab* at Discovery Channel's site, located at: *http://www.discovery-channel.ca/Showpage.aspx?sid=12767*.

Room Set-up

Set room with four chairs to form the seats in a cab.

Program Outline

1. Icebreaker: Choose a favorite in Chapter 3.

2. Form Teams: Tweens form teams of two or three and choose a team name.

3. Explain Discovery Channel's *Cash Cab*.

4. Decide which team is first.

    A. You can do paper, scissor, rock or draw numbers to determine which team goes first.

    B. The rest of the tweens waiting for their turn in the cab become audience members or pedestrians on the street.

    C. First team gets into the cab and the driver (librarian or person in charge of program) asks the team a series of up to five trivia questions in the allotted time of ten minutes.

5. Game Play

    A. Trivia questions are organized by subject and used at will, or they can be drawn out of a bucket or hat.

    B. Limit each cab ride to ten minutes, or how long you think would allow all teams to have a chance to play.

    C. At the end of the team's time limit, if they are still in the cab without three strikes, the ride is over and they have the option of trying for the bonus question.

    D. Each question is harder and worth more money.

    E. Money is handed out by the driver after each question is correctly answered.

    F. Dollar amounts for each question are $5, $10, $20, $50, and $100.

    G. The bonus question is difficult and the team risks losing all their money, or doubling if they decide to take the chance.

    H. If the team declines their bonus question, they leave the cab with the cash they have earned and wait for the other teams to take their ride.

    I. Teams get two "shout-outs," the chance to ask the audience/pedestrians for help.

    J. Teams get three strikes before they are booted out of the cab.

    K. Once kicked out, they lose all their money and return to the audience.

6. Award Prizes: If a team still has cash at the end of their ride, they can use the cash to buy candy and/or prizes you have on hand. Teams must total their cash and divide it by the number of team members evenly. Each individual team member then gets that much money to spend on prizes.

7. Clean up.

Materials Used

- Play money
- Trivia
- Prizes
- Candy

Budget

Approximately $20 for silly prizes and candy

General Comments

Select trivia for tweens carefully. You don't want to make it too hard; nor do you want it to be too easy. Check for trivia books in the children's section of your library and display during the program.

Neon New Year's Eve Party

Adults have heaps of New Year's Eve parties and kids can attend New Year's Eve story times. But what about tweens? Now those aged 10-14 can have their own harmless fun in the safety of their local library! Your party can really have any theme, but we recommend a "neon" or "glow in the dark" theme for some added fun. As with most parties, your imagination (and budget) is the limit. But in case you're not feeling particularly imaginative, we've included a few ideas for you to try!

Program Advertisement

Are you ready to PARTY???!! Countdown to the New Year in style...neon style that is! Throw on some bright neon clothes or accessories and join us for some glow in the dark fun. Show off your gangnam style dance moves and practice your moon walk! Prizes for the best neon outfit! For tweens ages 10-14.

Number of Spaces Available

30 (more if you have a large space available)

Program Preparation (2hours)

1. Select a variety of songs to play. Borrow the CDs from your collection and consolidate onto a single CD. Or, download songs from iTunes (*www.itunes.com*). Make sure the songs you choose do not contain any explicit lyrics.

2. Visit *www.youtube.com* to learn any dances that go along with the songs you've chosen. Tweens might know how to do some dances, but you'll need to teach them the others.

3. Pull a variety of CDs for display. This will help to tie the program into the promotion of the library collection.

4. Practice using the sound system (if applicable). It is important to note that while the music may seem loud in an empty room, once it is filled with chatting and laughing tweens, the volume will definitely have to be increased to the maximum level.

5. If your room is not very soundproof, notify other customers via signage that the library will be louder than normal during the program. This may help to reduce the number of upset customers who want to use the library for quiet study.

Songs to play...
- "Billie Jean"...Michael Jackson (for moonwalking)
- "Cha Cha Slide"...Casper
- "Chicken Dance/Little Bird Dance/BirdieZDance"... Werner Thomas
- "Gangnam Style"...Psy
- "The Loco-Motion"...Kylie Minogue
- "Macarena"...Los del Rio
- "Single Ladies (Put a Ring on It)"...Beyonce
- "The Twist"...Chubby Checker
- "YMCA"...The Village People
- "Around the World"...Daft Punk (for robot style dancing)

At a TWIG meeting or tween program, ask tweens what music they like to dance or listen to. Include a few of these at the party if the lyrics are appropriate.

6. Purchase or borrow a rotating disco ball light. These table top units plug into an electrical outlet and add some amazing ambience. Prices generally start at $20, but uses for the light are endless. Think future dance parties, story times, drawing attention to displays, and more!

7. Purchase New Year's Eve hats and noise makers. If you plan your programs well in advance, purchase these items when they are in the clearance bin on January 2!

8. Purchase glow sticks and/or glow bracelets, and glow-in-the-dark stickers.

9. Purchase prizes. If your budget is non-existent, use library promotional items like key chains, pens, and bags.

Room Set-up

An open area for dancing

Tables for refreshments and displays

Program Outline

1. Icebreaker: To make tweens feel more comfortable, especially in a dance environment, begin with an icebreaker from Chapter 3.

2. Hand out glow sticks and glow-in-the-dark stickers: If you are handing out glow necklaces, make it clear that tweens cannot twirl them around, as they are a hazard to other party goers.

3. Explain the rules: Make sure tweens know that just because the lights are dimmed, the same library rules apply. Encourage tweens to have fun dancing but to refrain from running or horseplay. Also explain that either you or another tween will be demonstrating dance moves, but it's up to the individual tweens to follow or just freestyle it! While there are behavior rules, there are no dance rules!

4. Let the dancing begin: Start by dimming the lights so everyone is less self-conscious. Before each song begins, you can ask if anyone wants to come up to the front of the room and lead the others by demonstrating the dance moves to that particular song. If no one volunteers, then you as a staff member are front and center! So bust a move and have fun!

5. Countdown to "midnight": Obviously this will not happen at midnight, so choose a time during the program where you will begin your countdown. But just before you start counting; hand out noisemakers so tweens can fully participate in the experience. You could hand the noisemakers out earlier in the program, but this could cause a lot of headaches for library staff who are running the program!

6. Dance off: After the "formal" portion of the program, have tweens form a large circle around the perimeter of the room. One at a time, tweens can take turns entering the circle to show off their dance moves. The tweens forming the circle can clap and cheer for the tweens in the middle. Because some tweens are shy, no one should be forced to enter the dance circle.

7. Refreshments: Tweens will get thirsty practicing all of their dance moves. Have some water or juice boxes available so no one gets dehydrated!

8. Award prizes for the best neon outfit.

9. Clean up.

Materials Used

- Glow sticks/ glow bracelets/ glow necklaces
- Glow-in-the-dark stickers
- New Year's Eve hats
- New Year's Eve noise makers
- A variety of music
- CD player or sound system
- Rotating disco ball light
- Refreshments

Budget

Approximately $75 (less if you don't purchase a disco ball, refreshments, or prizes)

General Comments

This is an amazingly fun program for tweens, but also for library staff! If you have a responsible group of tweens, this program should run super smoothly. If you have a more rowdy or trouble-some group, you may want to modify details of the party, adding a bit more structure or keeping more of the lights on. It's also important that you lead the dances, even if you don't really want to. For starters, tweens won't feel as dorky if you look like a dork, and secondly, it helps get everyone involved rather than standing at the sidelines not really knowing what to do!

Index

About the Authors

Tiffany Balducci, a former teen services librarian, is currently the Northview Branch librarian at Oshawa Public Libraries, where she has worked five years. She happily serves the White Pine Selection and Steering committees for the Ontario Library Association. She received her MLIS from Wayne State University and specializes in programming and class visits for public libraries. When she's not reading or librariaaning it up, Balducci enjoys watching reality television and spending time with her rescued cats and pug.

Brianne Wilkins-Bester is a former children's librarian, teen librarian, and branch manager who is currently taking a break from librarianship to pursue a venture in "modern homesteading." Realizing she wanted to be a librarian since the fourth grade, Wilkins-Bester received her MLIS from the University of Western Ontario, where she focused on management and public library courses. When not pursuing the profession, Wilkins-Bester finds delight in reading, gardening, and spending time with her family. Wilkins-Bester is also a proud ovarian cancer survivor.